The Christian as Minister

An Exploration Into the Meaning of God's Call to Ministry
and the Ways The United Methodist Church Offers
To Live Out That Call

Eighth Edition
2013

Meg Lassiat, editor

Contributors
Tom Carter
Bruce Fenner
Melissa Hinnen
Becky Louter
Mary Jane Pierce Norton
Melanie Overton
HiRho Park
Bridgette Young-Ross

HIGHER EDUCATION & MINISTRY
General Board of Higher Education and Ministry
THE UNITED METHODIST CHURCH

General Board of Higher Education and Ministry
The United Methodist Church
Nashville, Tennessee

The Christian as Minister

This resource is a compilation of information about the call to ministry and the avenues The United Methodist Church offers to live out that call. It is based in the concept of servant ministry and servant leadership presented by the Council of Bishops and affirmed by the General Conference.

Contents

Foreword

All Christians are ministers by virtue of their baptism. This book is an introduction into the meaning of God's call to ministry, the vision for that ministry, and the opportunities The United Methodist Church offers to live out that call.

In Chapter 2 you will read about several opportunities for service and offices in the church as a lay person or as licensed and ordained clergy. Some of these positions for servant leadership may be filled by either a lay or ordained person. Chapter 3 outlines steps and processes necessary to move into the roles described in this book.

As avenues for ministry, the positions are all related in that they offer the love of Christ to one another and the world in fulfilling the mission of the church. They are differentiated in their preparation for service, their structures of accountability, their length of commitment, and the specialized area of service.

Even though the General Board of Higher Education and Ministry has published this edition, *The Christian as Minister* would not have been complete without the cooperation and contribution of other general boards of The United Methodist Church which offer avenues and training for means of service in, and on behalf of, the church, both for lay and ordained ministries.

- Part of the General Board of Higher Education and Ministry's purpose is to prepare and assist those serving in ordained and licensed ministry.

- The General Board of Discipleship helps people to serve in discipleship around the world.
- The General Board of Global Ministries' responsibility in leadership is to encourage and support mission leadership throughout the church and world.

Categories of Servant Leadership Described in This Book

Lay Ministry
- Lay Leader, who serves as the primary representative of the laity in the local church, district, or annual conference.
- Lay Missioner, who works in a team to develop faith communities.
- Lay Servant Ministries, which give assistance and support to the program emphases of the church.
- Certified Lay Ministers, who enhance the quality of ministry and provide pastoral leadership under the authority of an elder, particularly to small membership churches.
- Deaconesses and home missioners, who are consecrated and commissioned to ministries of love, justice, and service, embodying the church in the world through a full-time vocation of servant ministry.

Licensed and Ordained Ministries
- Chaplains and Pastoral Counselors, who serve in specialized ministries of counseling.
- Deacons, who lead the church in the servanthood to which every Christian is called, relating the congregational life of the church to their ministries of compassion and justice in the world.
- Elders, who lead the church in preaching, the sacraments, administration, and ordering the life of the church for mission.
- Local Pastors, who provide pastoral leadership in local congregations under the authority of a license for pastoral ministry.

Both Lay and Ordained Opportunities
- Commissioned Mission Service, in which people serve in several areas of missionary service, both nationally and globally.

- Campus Ministers and Chaplains, who serve at United Methodist-related institutions and other colleges and universities.
- Certification in Specialized Ministries, in which people are professionally trained and certified in areas of ministry.

There are many settings where this resource may be useful besides an individual reading or a one-on-one conversation:

- High school, college, young adult, and adult groups could be guided through vocational exploration in Sunday, weekend, or retreat settings.
- In a Group Candidacy Mentoring setting or Orientation to Ministry event to discuss the different UM ministry settings.
- Under the guidance of the annual conference's vocational discernment coordinator as those discerning God's call meet to explore ministry options.
- College and university students may wish to explore the meaning of Christian vocation with a campus minister or a group of college students.
- Couples could read together and discuss what they learn from *The Christian as Minister*, since career and family decisions are often closely interrelated.
- Read the "Guidelines for Using the Text" and the "Guidelines for the Staff/Pastor-Parish Relations Committee" contained in Chapters 4 and 5 for other suggested uses.

On behalf of the editorial committee, it is our hope that this text will serve as a starting point for conversation as you begin exploring the many different ways you can respond to God's call in your life by serving in and on behalf of The United Methodist Church.

Yours in ministry,
Meg Lassiat
Director of Candidacy, Mentoring, and Conference Relations
Division of Ordained Ministry
General Board of Higher Education and Ministry

Acknowledgments

Meg Lassiat, Director of Candidacy, Mentoring, and Conference Relations, General Board of Higher Education and Ministry, has coordinated the revision of *The Christian as Minister*. We are grateful to Mary Jane Pierce Norton for coordinating the contributions from the General Board of Discipleship; to Melissa Hinnen at the General Board of Global Ministries; to Becky Louter at United Methodist Women, and Tom Carter, Bruce Fenner, Melanie Overton, HiRho Park, and Bridgette Young-Ross at the General Board of Higher Education and Ministry for their careful writing, review, and preparation of this text.

Thanks also to the Office of Interpretation, specifically Terri Hiers and Vicki Brown for their editorial assistance; and to Richard A. Hunt, author of the first edition. Many of his thoughts and ideas were retained in this revision.

The Christian as Minister (ISBN 978-0-938162-63-6, $9.99 each) is available from Cokesbury.com or by calling 1-800-673-1789.

Chapter One
The Christian Call to Servant Ministry

The Mission and Ministry of the Church

Living in the twenty-first century has a compelling quality that evokes reflection on what has been and from where we have come. It also propels us forward to possibilities for the future and what can be.

To be sure, this time in history presents many changes and shifting priorities. Economic, social, and political forces contribute to the complexity of our society, and this diversity challenges us to examine our relationship, calling, and work in new ways. The church is there to help us reflect and respond to these changes through the lens of our faith.

The church is where we learn about our faith, grow in it, and define our beliefs, which influence our actions, behaviors, and the way we live our lives. As a faith community, however, the church is not merely a human institution. It is the community where we also experience a relationship with God — a forgiving and transformative relationship founded on God's creative and unmerited love, the continuing redemptive grace of Jesus Christ, and the sustaining guidance of the

A somber crowd observes an interfaith World Aids Day memorial service in Baton Rouge, La. The service was organized by the Louisiana Annual Conference.

Holy Spirit. Therefore, the church embodies both the ambiguities of life and the unquestionable continuing presence of Jesus the Christ.

The church is divine gift coupled with human response. The church cannot be seen apart from its community. When that community is faithful, it transforms and liberates people and institutions from personal and social forms of sin. Freedom and transformation are the critical work of the church in our time — the mission and ministry of the church.

Rationale for Our Mission

The mission of the church is to make disciples of Jesus Christ by proclaiming the good news of God's grace . . . thus seeking the fulfillment of God's reign and realm in the world. The fulfillment of God's reign and realm in the world is the vision Scripture holds before us. The United Methodist Church affirms that Jesus Christ is the Son of God, the Savior of the world, and the Lord of all. We respect persons of all religious faiths and we defend religious freedom for all persons. Jesus' words in Matthew provide the Church

10

with our mission: "Therefore, go and make disciples of all na-
tions, baptizing them in the name of the Father and of the Son
and of the Holy Spirit, teaching them to obey everything that I've
commanded you...." (28:19-20).

This mission is our grace-filled response to the Reign of God in
the world announced by Jesus. God's grace is active everywhere,
at all times, carrying out this purpose as revealed in the Bible. It
is expressed in God's covenant with Abraham and Sarah, in the
Exodus of Israel from Egypt, and in the ministry of the prophets.
It is fully embodied in the life, death, and resurrection of Jesus
Christ. It is experienced in the ongoing creation of a new people
by the Holy Spirit.

John Wesley, Phillip Otterbein, Jacob Albright, and our other
spiritual forbearers understood this mission in this way. When-
ever United Methodism has had a clear sense of mission, God has
used our church to save persons, heal relationships, transform
social structures, and spread spiritual holiness, thereby changing
the world. In order to be truly alive, we embrace Jesus' mandate
to . . . make disciples of all peoples (Book of Discipline).

In the midst of our world community, beset by brokenness, the
church offers a vision of peace, wholeness, and unity which God
wills for all creation. It is this vision and this mission that gives
the church focus and drive, and which invigorates and guides the
church and its people.

Reflection

- In what ways have you experienced the church as a faith community in your life?
- In what ways have you experienced the church as a response
  to the societal and political forces which exclude, alienate, and
  marginalize?
- What is your understanding of the church's mission?

Baptism and Call

Baptism is God's gift of unmerited grace through the Holy Spirit. It is an incorporation into Christ which marks the entrance of each person into the church and its ministry (Romans 6:3, 4, 18).

As United Methodists we believe that when we are baptized, we are called into ministry on behalf of Christ. The baptism liturgy tells us that "through baptism, (we) are incorporated by the Holy Spirit into God's new creation and made to share in Christ's royal priesthood."[1]

United Methodists believe all people have a place among the people of God and are to be afforded the same holy privileges, regardless of age. When baptized as infants, children are to be nurtured in the faith and led to personal acceptance of Christ. Upon profession of faith in Christ, they confirm their baptism and acknowledge their place as growing disciples in the ministry of Christ.

New Jersey pastor, the Rev. Myrna Bethke, holds baby Elizabeth Anne Binder on the day of her Baptism.

This important aspect of the liturgy serves to remind all that, through baptism and upon profession of faith — regardless of age, stage in life, or particular gifts and talents — our lives on this earth are to be visible extensions of the life and ministry of Jesus. We are the hands, the feet, the arms, the legs, the mind, the heart — the manifestation of Christ in the world.

Through baptism we are acknowledged and incorporated into God's family and God's vision for a new creation and called to be a part of Christ's mission and ministry. The way each person responds to that call may lead to a time of reflection and deliberation about how God intends one to live out a Christian vocation. Vocation is defined by *The Random House College Dictionary* as a function or station in life to which one is called by God."[2]

The Gospel According to Matthew chronicles the significance of Jesus' baptism and his relationship with God, and signals the beginning of his mission and ministry — his vocation.

> *When Jesus was baptized, he immediately came up out of the water. Heaven was opened to him, and he saw the Spirit of God coming down like a dove and resting on him. A voice from heaven said, 'This is my Son whom I dearly love; I find happiness in him' (Matthew 3:16-17).*

The baptism of Jesus Christ was a significant act, because it publicly declared God's blessing and anointing. It was a commissioning — an empowering act of grace through the work of the Holy Spirit. By virtue of our own baptism, we too are commissioned, anointed, and empowered to continue the ministry that Jesus started when he walked this earth. That makes all baptized persons ministers.

That God calls all to witness and service cannot be denied. However, the kind of witness and the kind of service to which God calls is a far more difficult question to answer. This, again, is the question of vocation — the place where God's will for our lives and our obedience come together in the fulfillment of our purpose for being.

If you are exploring how God is calling you to live out Christ's ministry and vision, some of your anxiety may be addressed by carefully studying Jesus' struggle with his vocation and calling. There was a time in his life when Jesus did not know that he was to bear the history of God in a special way, a time when his vocation in life was not clearly understood. He struggled with who he was in relationship to God, and what it was that God intended for him to do. The Holy Spirit aided him in that discovery process. In his baptism, Jesus was revealed to be God's beloved son, and was then led into the wilderness to struggle with the identity and vocation to which God was calling him.

Even after Jesus had clarified his calling, it was not always affirmed by the people of God. Listen to this account of his ministry in the synagogue at Nazareth.

> Jesus went to Nazareth, where he had been raised. On the Sabbath he went to the synagogue as he normally did and stood up to read. The synagogue assistant gave him the scroll from the prophet Isaiah. He unrolled the scroll and found the place where it was written: "The Spirit of the Lord is upon me, because the Lord has anointed me. He has sent me to preach good news to the poor, to proclaim release to the prisoners and recovery of sight to the blind, to liberate the oppressed, and to proclaim the year of the Lord's favor." He rolled up the scroll, gave it back to the synagogue assistant, and sat down. Every eye in the synagogue was fixed on him. He began to explain to them, "Today, this scripture has been fulfilled just as you heard it." Everyone was raving about Jesus, so impressed were they by the gracious words flowing from his lips. They said, "This is Joseph's son, isn't it?" Then Jesus said to them, "Undoubtedly, you will quote this saying to me: 'Doctor, heal yourself. Do here in your hometown what we've heard you did in Capernaum.'" He said, "I assure you that no prophet is welcome in the prophet's hometown...." When they heard this, everyone in the synagogue was filled with anger. They rose up and ran him out of town. They led him to the crest of the hill on which their town had been built so that they could throw him off the cliff. But he passed through the crowd and went on his way. (Luke 4:16-24; 28-30).

Christ's vocation was and is radically different than your vocation. Nevertheless, there is a relationship between his calling and yours. It is not accidental that you may be able to identify with elements in Jesus' baptism, wilderness journey, and ministry. His struggle with vocational choice was as real as yours.

In a way, your vocation in life grows out of his because Christ invites you, through the Holy Spirit, to share in God's story by witnessing to its reality in your life and living it out through your actions.

Like Christ and the Apostles and the host of saints who have gone before you in the faith, you are called to discover the meaning of your vocation through the gospel stories. While the ways in which you tell it and the service you render in obedience to God's will differ from all others who surround you in the faith, you will find in that vocation, and only there, a true sense of who you are in relationship to God and who it is that you were meant to become. Gilbert Meilaender, professor of theology at Valparaiso University, writes in an article on vocation in the November 2000 edition of *The Christian Century:* "It is only by hearing, answering, and participating in the divine calling that I can come to know who I am. We are not who we think we are; we are who God calls us to be."[3]

Reflection

- As part of Christ's family, signified by your baptism, what does being a minister to the world in Christ's name mean to you?
- What work would God have you do in the name of Christ, for the sake of the world?
- To what kind of ministry might God call you that would require your total obedience?

Vocation and Servant Leadership[4]

Few people today enter the same occupation or line of work as their parents. Some drift into an occupation or follow the advice or pressure of parents or teachers or friends. The more deliberate may choose an occupation by considering what they do best or what they most enjoy doing. If they are systematic, they may consider the pros and cons of various trades or professions and study job listings to make a more deliberate choice.

Responding to a call to a particular occupation, career or vocation is another way of determining what one will do for one's lifework. Even though a call to a vocation might have elements listed in the preceding paragraph, it is also something above and beyond all of them.

15

Latonja Tucker paints an exterior wall at Bethany United Methodist Church in New Orleans, which was damaged by floodwaters from Hurricane Katrina.

This kind of call is not something a person responds to by default or under social pressure, or entirely by free choice. This call implies a caller. The Caller is God. *The Random House College Dictionary* lists as one definition of call: a "mystic experience of divine appointment to a vocation or service. . . ." [5] So determining one's vocation is more than fulfilling a personal dream; it is responding to God to become who and what God calls you to be. One gets to vocation through God's call.

The concept of a call by God can historically and biblically be applied to three distinct experiences.

- In the beginning, God called people into being. The word call is used here to refer to an important dimension of our relationship to God — a call that we share with all of humanity.
- Then God, through Jesus, calls persons to accept God's grace. People respond to this call by their commitment to Christ and his ministry. This is what binds us with all other Christians in the ministry of all believers.

- God also calls some to a particular form of servant leadership within the church. Empowered and guided by the Holy Spirit, these individuals respond to that call through a life-changing and often lifelong commitment to service and ministry.

The distinction between these calls, particularly the last two, is important. Every Christian is called to follow Christ in her or his walk of life wherever he or she is — the ministry of all believers. For those who respond to a particular form of servant leadership, the word "call" expresses something that is uniquely different for each individual and something that hopefully leads to a vocation which theologian Frederick Buechner described as where one's greatest joy meets the world's greatest need.

Any type of call, sudden or gradual, needs time for reflecting, questioning and testing. To continue exploring your call and its meaning for your vocation, talk with your pastor or another United Methodist minister or church leader.

The Meaning of Servant Leadership

The United Methodist Church holds that servant leadership is at the heart of ministry and leadership, and that God's call to ministry is responded to by an individual, but confirmed by the church community. Those responding to a call to ministry (whether lay, licensed, or ordained) must embody Christ's teachings and demonstrate their gifts for ministry and promise for future usefulness.

Some might argue that servant leadership is a contradiction of terms. In order to explore the role of the servant leader more fully, look at the origin of the use of the term in our society and reflect on the most exemplary biblical servant leader of all time — Jesus Christ.

The term servant leadership was coined almost 30 years ago, in the business world, by Robert K. Greenleaf, director of Management Research at AT&T, during the time of the Vietnam War, the political corruptness of Watergate, and Civil Rights unrest. His inspiration for this conception came from a novel by Hermann Hesse, a German poet and novelist, called *Journey to the East*.

"In this story we see a band of men on a mythical journey. . . . The central figure of the story is Leo who accompanies the party as the servant who does their menial chores, but who also sustains them with his spirit and his song. He is a person of extraordinary presence. All goes well until Leo disappears. Then the group falls into disarray and the journey is abandoned. They cannot make it without the servant Leo. The narrator, one of the party, after some years of wandering, finds Leo and is taken into the Order that had sponsored the [original] journey. There he discovers that Leo, whom he had known first as servant, was in fact the titular head of the Order, its guiding spirit, a great and noble leader." [6]

To Greenleaf, this story illustrated that "the great leader is seen as servant first." The difference between servant-first and leader-first "manifests itself in the care taken by the servant-first to make sure that other people's highest priority needs are being served. The best test is: do those served grow as persons; do they, while being served, become healthier, wiser freer, more autonomous." [7]

In most societies, including present day North America, many people are socialized or programmed, as it were, to become either servants or leaders. Through cultural conditioning or through the operation of social structures some may be more predisposed to leadership roles, others to servant roles. In order to become a servant leader, a person must recognize her or his own predisposition. Those who see themselves as servants will need to learn to exercise leadership because in God's realm the effective servant often becomes a leader. Those who see themselves as leaders need to learn how to serve, because in God's realm the real leaders are those who serve most effectively. [8]

Servant Leadership in the Connectional Church

There is but one ministry in Christ, but there are diverse gifts and evidences of God's grace in the body of Christ (Ephesians 4:4-16).

Through incorporation into the church, by baptism, people are connected to one another through Christ no matter what their role in ministry is. This connection shares a common faith tradition, a common mission through Christ, and a common spirit that informs United Methodist beliefs and practices. The connectionalism of the church provides a system that enables congregations and other min-

Muyombo Mande, a delegate from the Democratic Republic of Congo, prays with other participants during the April 24 opening worship service of the 2012 United Methodist General Conference.

United Methodists gathered for General Conference 2012 in Tampa, Fla.

istry settings to "make disciples of Jesus Christ for the transformation of the world." Through this connection, the whole United Methodist Church is able to respond faithfully to its mission.

The pattern for this connectional servant ministry is presented in the biblical beginning of the early church. In Acts 6, we see that the apostles led in prayer, teaching, and preaching and ordered the community's life. They also established leadership for the ministry of service and provided ways for those new in the faith to hear and learn the gospel. They developed a system to ensure that the concerns of the world would be cared for, and authorized certain people in the ministries of service.

Our eighteenth century forebears in the faith reaffirmed the ancient Christian practices found in the early church even as they applied them anew in their own circumstances. Just as the early Christian church affirmed many different avenues for service and leadership, The United Methodist Church affirms and makes available many expressions of lay, licensed, and ordained ministry as people respond to God's call within the United Methodist connectional structure.

Reflection

- What means are you using to discover the lifework or vocation that you believe God intends for you?
- What are the ways you can lead people in your community or peer group to serve the needs that surround you?
- Do you feel that God may be calling you to be a servant leader? In what ways?
- What are questions that you have about different categories of ministry?

Notes

1. *The United Methodist Hymnal: Book of United Methodist Worship* (Nashville: The United Methodist Publishing House), p. 37.
2. *The Random House College Dictionary Revised Edition*, 1988, s.v. "vocation."
3. Gilbert Meilaender, "Divine Summons," in The Christian Century, November 2000 (Chicago: Christian Century Foundation), p. 1112.
4. Most of the following section is adapted from *The Call to Servant Leadership* by Simon Parker. (Nashville: Division of Diaconal Ministry, General Board of Higher Education and Ministry, The United Methodist Church, 1998), pp. 7-8.
5. *The Random House College Dictionary Revised Edition*, 1988, s.v. "call."
6. Robert K. Greenleaf, *Servant As Leader* (Newton Center: Robert K. Greenleaf Center, 1973), p. 1.
7. Ibid., pp. 2, 7.
8. This paragraph is adapted from Simon Parker, *The Call to Servant Leadership*, by Simon Parker, pp. 19-20.

Chapter Two
Images of Servant Leadership

Young People in Ministry

Everybody can be great, because everybody can serve. You don't have to have a college degree to serve. You don't have to make your subject and your verb agree to serve. You don't have to know about Plato and Aristotle to serve. You don't have to know Einstein's "Theory of Relativity" to serve. You don't have to know the Second Theory of Thermal Dynamics in Physics to serve. You only need a heart full of grace, a soul generated by love, and you can be that servant.

—*The Rev. Dr. Martin Luther King Jr.*[1]

God's call takes many forms and people hear God's call differently; therefore, people find many different ways to respond to God's call. Because we are called, God shows us places and ways to serve. The only requirement is being available to God and answering God's call.

Students attending Imagine What's NEXT, an event meant to challenge and inspire college students to consider and plan the next faithful steps for their vocations, their communities, the church, and the world wrote their hopes and dreams for their faith communities and The United Methodist Church on foam boards the final day of the event.

Ben was traveling with his sixth grade confirmation class the weekend after the September 11, 2001, terrorist attacks on the World Trade Center. Overwhelmed by his desire to help children whose parents had been injured or killed, he suggested sending stuffed animals to these children as one way to provide comfort. Ben shared his idea with the other confirmation students and they decided to help. Members of the class talked with students at several local schools and announced the need for stuffed animals at church, through church mailings, and on the church website. For the next two weeks, stuffed animals were collected, both at the schools and at the church. When the class met to sort the toys and ship them to New York, they discovered more than 1,000 stuffed animals had been collected! They were given to law enforcement officers, social workers, and area churches to share with children most directly affected by the attacks.

t age 16, Tiffany was the president of her youth group. She was a leader among her peers and also attended a number of church council meetings. Both youth and adult members of the congregation admired and followed Tiffany's leadership. One day the pastor at her church asked to meet so that they could discuss Tiffany's ministry. At their meeting, the pastor said, "I'm so glad that you've decided to be a minister!" A look of concern crossed Tiffany's face. "I never told Rev. Williams I'd be a minister," Tiffany thought. "Doesn't she know I want to be a doctor? Besides, I'm only 16. I don't feel called to be a minister." Noticing Tiffany's confusion, Williams further explained, "When we take our baptism seriously and follow God's call to be a disciple of Jesus Christ, we are ministers — regardless of age, gender or our career plans. You may be called to be a pastor like I am, or your ministry may be in the hospital like you dream. Either way, I'm excited that you've been called to serve!"

<hr/>

s Hannah boarded the plane to leave on her second trip to Zimbabwe, she couldn't help but reflect on what the last year had meant for her. During the summer between her junior and senior years in high school, she traveled to Zimbabwe with her church's youth group to work with children at the Fairfield Children's Home in Old Mutare, Zimbabwe. While at the orphanage Hannah played with the children, shared laughter and smiles with them, and developed relationships with the adult workers — relationships that continued to make an impression on her once she returned to the United States. She knew she would return to Mutare. Hannah shared the story of her time in Zimbabwe with friends at her high school and soon decided to lead a trip back there so her friends could see and experience some of the same things she had. Eighteen other classmates and friends joined the group and they began preparations for their upcoming trip. Hannah organized the trip, made travel arrangements, and worked tirelessly helping the group to raise funds. She stayed in contact with the people at Fairfield and planned what the group would do during their visit. Additionally, she worked with her school administrators to establish an ongoing sponsorship program to provide needed food and medical supplies for the children. She learned a lot in the process and knew she was making a difference — not only with the children at the Fairfield Orphanage, but with her friends who would soon get to meet the people at Fairfield and experience Zimbabwe firsthand. She was excited to return and knew this would not be the last time she would visit.

It is clear that Mary, the mother of Jesus, had no intention to be used by God in such an amazing way. It probably never crossed her young mind that she would have a son who could be one of the teachers in the temple, or a traveling pastor. Not to mention that she would be an instrument to help change the world. Yet, when God called on her to carry and give birth to Jesus, her response was: "I am the Lord's servant. Let it be with me just as you have said" (Luke 1:38). Without ordination or formal education, Mary, at a young age, answered God's call to serve.

Servant leadership is both a gift and task. God's grace comes to us as a gift through our response to serve. At the same time, we know that we are being called to a demanding task. When you join the church, you answer a call from God. You say "yes" to God's grace, to becoming part of a community of Christians, and to serving others on behalf of Jesus Christ.

Reflection

- What image comes to your mind when you ask: How is God calling me to respond as a baptized Christian?
- How have you led in your community, whether in school or another setting?
- What experiences have you had that influence the way you answer a call from God which may lead to a vocation in the church?
- Visit www.explorecalling.org for information on calling and identifying your spiritual gifts.

Volunteers Forrest Mayer (left) and Chris Grier sort donated clothing at the Absentee Shawnee Resource Center in Little Axe, Okla., that served as a relief center after tornadoes in Oklahoma in 2013.

The Ministry of the Laity

The Call

The heart of Christian ministry is to share Christ's love in the world. The ministry of the laity is a frontline ministry because lay people have direct access to the community and the world through their jobs and activities.

All of the people of God are called to be faithful in their ministry. Church members are the church made visible in the world and are called to share the gospel of Jesus Christ within and beyond the church community. This responsibility cannot be delegated nor can it be evaded. If Christians are not faithful in ministry, the church will lose its impact on the world.

As members of the body of Christ, we are all are gifted for service and have received different gifts for ministry. "There are different spiritual gifts but the same Spirit..." (1 Corinthians 12:4). It is liberating to realize that each one of us is called to ministry and that each one's ministry is just as important as the other's. It is essential to realize this important fact and live out ministry as we have been gifted and called — whether it is in the factory, or the hospital; at work or at home; in the church, or in the community. Christ has called and we answer by serving to the best of our ability.

Privilege and Responsibility

The call to ministry is both a privilege and a responsibility. We are privileged to be in relationship with God. It is a privilege to be part of a "holy nation, a people who are God's own possession." Those called to ministry are called to "speak of the wonderful acts of the one who called [us] out of darkness into his amazing light" (1 Peter 2:9). And it is a privilege to speak of God's wonderful acts.

It is also a responsibility. Christians respond to God's call by holy living and obedience to Christ. Holy living inspires intentional growth and nurturing. Each must continue to grow spiritually, to mature in the Christian life in order to fully engage in the ministry of all Christians.

John Wesley established The General Rules for the Societies who met together to pray, worship, and watch over one another in love. These rules included ways to accomplish the task of loving and serving others. First, by doing no harm and by avoiding evil of every kind. Second, by doing good of every possible sort, and as far as possible to all persons. Third, by attending upon all the ordinances of God which are the practices by which we stay connected to God, grow in faith and in the ability to love — the means of grace (see General Rules, *Book of Discipline*).

What does servant leadership look like in an everyday life?

Here are a few examples:

Naomi is a nurse who has felt God's call on her life. She lives out that call in her work every day trying to treat her co-workers, supervisor, and patients the way Jesus would treat them. She goes out of her way to perform acts of kindness and she offers to pray for people she meets who are hurting. Outside the workplace she seeks ways to grow spiritually through prayer, Bible study, and worship, and to develop the sense of call in her life. Because of her deepened spirituality she has the courage to pray with patients and co-workers as well as for them. She volunteers to visit church members who are homebound or in the hospital. She has started a prayer ministry in her church to help others realize the power and importance of prayer.

Brian works as an electrician. He finds ways to befriend others, share his faith story, and invite them to church. Brian is obedient to Christ in his daily life by showing concern for his fellow workers. He refuses to cut corners or be dishonest with his employer. Brian walks the talk. Outside of work he is active in prison ministry and serves as a volunteer at the local prison in order to make a difference in the lives of the inmates and prison personnel. At church he leads a team to provide a free community Christmas meal. He also leads mission trips within the United States and to other countries where he uses his skills to work with members of these communities as they build affordable housing for residents.

Beth has a full-time job as wife and mother. Her ministry in daily life is providing nourishing meals, clean laundry, and living conditions for her family. She sees this as her service to God and her vocation. She leads in her district and annual conference where she teaches classes to help other laity improve their leadership and ministry skills. She encourages people to be involved by using their skills to serve others. This has led many people to serve in community ministries such as serving lunch at the homeless shelter or delivering Meals on Wheels. Beth wants others to feel welcome in her church so she often serves as a greeter at worship services.

ee is an accountant who ministers in his work by using ethical practices in his company and dealing honestly with his employees and clients. He devotes time in the community to coaching a Little League baseball team and serves as an example to other coaches of Christ's love for children. As a member of his church's finance committee, Lee tries to ensure that the meetings are more than church business by encouraging holy conferencing and Christian fellowship. He is part of a weekly covenant group that prays for each other and holds each other accountable for their discipleship.

All of these people are in vital ministry. They demonstrate servant ministry and leadership in their daily work lives, their families, communities, churches, and in the world.

Now when the Human One comes in his majesty and all his angels are with him, he will sit on his majestic throne. All the nations will be gathered in front of him. He will separate them from each other, just as a shepherd separates the sheep from the goats. He will put the sheep on his right side. But the goats he will put on his left. "Then the king will say to those on his right, "Come, you who will receive good things from my Father. Inherit the kingdom that was prepared for you before the world began. I was hungry and you gave me food to eat. I was thirsty and you gave me a drink. I was a stranger and you welcomed me. I was naked and you gave me clothes to wear. I was sick and you took care of me. I was in prison and you visited me."

Then those who are righteous will reply to him, "Lord, when did we see you hungry and feed you, or thirsty and give you a drink? When did we see you as a stranger and welcome you, or naked and give you clothes to wear? When did we see you sick or in prison and visit you?

Then the king will reply to them, "I assure you that when you have done it for one of the least of these brothers and sisters of mine, you have done it for me" (Matthew 25:31-40).

Reflection

- How have you been obedient to the call to servant ministry?
- In what ways can you invest your time and talents for ministry in the name of Christ?
- What opportunities do you have in your everyday life to be in ministry?

The Ministry of the Deaconess and Home Missioner

Deaconesses, who are laywomen, and home missioners, who are laymen, are professionally trained persons who have been led by the Holy Spirit to devote their lives to Christ-like service under the authority of the church. They are approved through a process established by United Methodist Women, consecrated and commissioned by a bishop to serve in settings approved by the board of directors of United Methodist Women. They shall have a continuing relationship to The United Methodist Church through United Methodist Women (*Book of Discipline*).

The Office of Deaconess was first authorized in 1888 by the General Conference of The Methodist Episcopal Church and was subsequently authorized in each of the predecessor organizations that now compose The United Methodist Church. It offered laywomen the opportunity to serve in a lifetime relationship of servant ministry. The relationship of home missioner was created by the 2004 General Conference, and provides laymen with this same opportunity.

Deaconesses and home missioners function as a lay diaconal order within The United Methodist Church. They serve in diverse forms of service directed toward the world to make Jesus Christ known in the fullness of his ministry and mission. The ministries of deaconesses and home missioners focus on:

- Alleviating suffering;
- Eradicating causes of injustice and all that robs life of dignity and worth;
- Facilitating the development of full human potential; and

- Sharing in building global community through the church universal.

Full-time service is the norm for those who serve as a deaconess or home missioners. This means that one's entire vocational time is devoted to the work of ministry where one is appointed by the bishop.

Deaconesses and home missioners form a covenant community that is rooted in Scripture, informed by history, driven by mission, is ecumenical in scope, and global in outreach. These are laity who have responded to God's call in their lives and are consecrated and commissioned to be in a lifetime continuing relationship with The United Methodist Church. They are appointed to full-time ministries of love, justice, and service in a church-related vocation or helping profession. Deaconesses and home missioners serve in a diversity of contexts including prisons, health care facilities, schools and universities, church agencies, shelters, and community centers. Their ministries encompass a wide range of social justice concerns including environmental justice, immigration, poverty, homelessness, peace with justice, refugees, women and children, youth and families, and senior adults.

Deaconess and Home Missioner
Ministries of Love, Justice, and Service

Rosa has been involved with a drop-in center for more than a decade and now serves as its executive director. The center is a day shelter for people who are homeless, offers a food pantry, and also has staff who provide case management and advocacy services for clients in need. She heard God's call to service when she was young but did not know how to respond. Her pastor preached on God's call and she realized she had been denying God's call in her own life. The pastor encouraged her to explore the deaconess relationship, so she attended a discernment event. Through a weekend of sharing and praying, Rosa felt a sense of belonging to the deaconess and home missioner community. As a deaconess, she now answers the call to alleviate suffering and facilitate the development of full human potential through her work with homeless, marginalized, and low-in-come families. She now leads the drop-in center, where people in need can go daily to cook a meal, clean their clothes, shower, and get connected with programs and services that will help them get back on their feet.

❧

Esther is called to promote healthy lifestyles with racial-ethnic populations. She answers her call with a mixture of parish nursing and community organizing. Healthy lifestyles in her congregation include a wellness program and a mentoring program for teenage girls. Her coordination of health and wellness services through the church serves those who are often disenfranchised by health care systems. The mentor program helps teenage girls raise their ACT scores and gives them a chance at better opportunities in life. She reaches beyond her congregation and into the surrounding neighborhood serving as an advocate for the homeless and oppressed, promoting voter registration, and educating and empowering citizens against crime. Her ministry developed out of her discernment to become a deaconess. When she was forced into early retirement, she found new life through the deaconess and home missioner community where her gifts for public health service were celebrated and lifted up as an answer to God's call.

❧

George is a home missioner who was working with a university agricultural department. Upon seeing how much food rotted in fields after large mechanical harvests, he felt called to start a new ministry that would get that surplus food to people who needed it. He has now organized his own ministry with gleaners and volunteers who harvest this food and donate it to food banks, soup kitchens, and local food pantries. His ministry distributes an average of 82,000 pounds of fresh vegetables each year. Just as important as providing healthy, nutritious food for the hungry, George is building relationships with farmers and volunteers so that excitement and passion for this ministry will continue for years to come.

onnie is a chaplain and coordinator of pastoral care for a large hospital. What she looks forward to most are her daily visits with patients. She helps them adjust to hospital routines while easing pain, loneliness, and anxiety. It is a great privilege to be a part of these patients' lives while they are in the hospital. She credits her current sense of fulfillment in living out her call to her discernment process prior to becoming a deaconess. It was through that process that her interest in medicine was reawakened and she found a connection between her seminary training and hospital chaplaincy. She knew she had answered her call when she felt an all-encompassing peace. Because she is living out her calling, she finds that God provides courage, energy, and wisdom to support her in her ministry.

arah ministers through music. She serves in two ministry settings: in a hospital and in a residential treatment facility for veterans. For those patients in the hospital, her music provides comfort and therapy in times of pain and healing. Her ministry with veterans is equally as rewarding. She teaches piano and guitar, helping those who are learning for the first time or becoming reacquainted with the instruments after their time in service. As part of her teaching, she organizes opportunities for her students to perform and lead sing-alongs in the waiting rooms of the nearby veteran's hospital—a setting that is familiar to most of them. They embrace these opportunities to begin giving back to others while they are still healing from the physical and emotional wounds of war.

ohn coordinates volunteers for a large relief organization responsible for helping those who have been affected by natural disasters. A retired civil engineer, this is his second career. It was during a mission trip to Honduras that John heard God's call to ministry in relief missions. It was an experience that opened his eyes to God's glory, and he is committed to helping others have similar experiences. When an elderly gentleman shares with him a profound experience from volunteering, he knows he is answering God's call for him as a home missioner.

Reflection

- How do you relate today's most pressing social justice issues with the mission of The United Methodist Church, to make disciples of Jesus Christ for the transformation of the world?
- Name one social justice issue that is important to you. What would it be like to devote your life to a full-time ministry of service that addresses this issue?
- Deaconesses and home missioners serve in diverse ministries, guided by Christ's mandates to alleviate suffering, eradicate causes of injustice and all that robs life of dignity and worth, facilitate the development of full human potential, and share in building global community through the church universal. Does your experience of call relate to these mandates?

The Ministry of the Deacon

Within the people of God, some persons are called to the ministry of deacon. The words deacon, deaconess, and diaconate all spring from a common Greek root–*diakonos*, or "servant," and *diakonia*, or "service." Very early in its history the church instituted an order for deacons to lead the church in servant ministry especially related to ministries that embody compassion and justice. Those who are called to serve as a deacon commit to a lifetime of servant leadership that is authorized by the church. They are ordained by a bishop.

Deacons fulfill servant ministry in the world and lead the church in relating the gathered life of Christians to their ministries in the world. . . . [They] give leadership in the church's life: in the teaching and proclamation of the Word; in worship, and in assisting the elders in the administration of the sacraments of baptism and the Lord's

Supper; in forming and nurturing disciples; in conducting marriages and burying the dead; in the congregation's mission to the world; and in leading the congregation in interpreting the needs, concerns, and hopes of the world.[2]

The role of the ordained deacon is as diverse as the world's needs. Following in the long history of diaconal workers, a deacon's call to word, service, compassion, and justice is lived out in a variety of ways. But it is always focused on providing servant leadership in one or more of the following:

- leading the church in its servant ministry by the formation of disciples and connectional outreach
- giving leadership to a direct service ministry beyond the local church
- giving leadership in worship and assisting in the sacraments of baptism and Holy Communion
- teaching and proclaiming the word directly or living out the word of Jesus' love and justice through action and deed.

Deacons serve in multiple settings:

- a local church
- a social service agency affiliated with the UMC
- an annual conference or general agency of the church
- an organization or ministry beyond the local church that responds to the needs of the community

Deacons are accountable to the annual conference and the bishop, and also to their primary setting in ministry. They must complete advanced theological education and train to serve in a specialized area of ministry. No matter where they serve, all deacons will always be affiliated with a local congregation helping to lead them in their servant ministry.

Deacons Serving in A Variety of Ministry Settings

Judith's passion for mission work dominates her work as a deacon associate at a local United Methodist Church. She helps oversee the 4,000-member church's adult ministries, including helping to lead a contemporary worship service, planning events and steward-ship campaigns, organizing Bible studies and small group ministries, and leading 260 singles ranging in age from 24 to 82 representing at least eight denominations. Divided into older and younger groups, the singles ministry offers Sunday morning classes, social activities, weekly Bible studies, retreats, and mission opportunities. With her support and guidance, the singles ministry and church-at-large has supported missionaries, traveled to Costa Rica and Mexico on mission trips, provided necessities for a nearby family shelter, collected items for the Society of Saint Stephens, and built homes for private sector initiatives.

J im has responded to the call to be a deacon as a social worker with seminary training and serves as the director of a United Methodist children's home. This agency has become a major pro-

The Rev. Lillian Smith, an elder, presides at Holy Communion, assisted by the Rev. David Dodge, a deacon.

vider of foster care for children who have been abandoned or have been physically or sexually abused. Jim notes that it is in the midst of suffering and oppression that the embodiment of the ministry of Jesus Christ needs to be present. He is connected with not one, but all the churches in the area, to interpret the tremendous need that exists in our society to give hope to our children. He incarnates the passage of Matthew 25:40 that says, "I assure you that when you have done it for one of the least of these brothers and sisters of mine, you have done it for me."

Mary is a deacon who has combined her training as a counselor with theological education to respond to her call to ministry. She serves as director of a crisis intervention center and believes that her work is an extension of the ministry of Jesus Christ and therefore of the church. In her office, she responds to crisis phone calls from people who are suffering with depression or who face problems in their lives and need to talk with someone who shows care and concern. She is committed to connecting the needs of the community and the gifts and talents of the congregation where she serves.

The area of health care is the setting for Naomi's ministry. She serves as a parish nurse to fulfill her call to deacon's ministry. In her community there are many older adults who need the services of a nurse. Naomi combines her licensed nursing skills with pastoral care and theological education to become a presence of the Body of Christ, the church, with the people.

Dean has been appointed as deacon to coordinate and mobilize a local church outreach ministry. He surveys the community's needs and determines how the congregation can respond. He knows the gifts, talents, and abilities of those in the congregation

The Rev. April Casperson, right, a deacon, assists during opening worship at the 2012 United Methodist General Conference in Tampa, Fla. Also shown, from left: Bishops Larry Goodpaster, Peggy Johnson, Rosemarie Wenner and João Somane Machado.

and how they can make a significant presence and difference in the community through their involvement in homeless ministries, hospice programs, Meals on Wheels, respite care, Habitat for Humanity, prison ministries, halfway houses, shelter for battered women, and the care program for patients with HIV/AIDS. He sees the importance of the interrelatedness of the community and the congregation. His call is to bring into reality John Wesley's statement, "The world is my parish."

Joan says she is called by God to minister with individuals who believe God does not love them. She started a ministry with pregnant women to serve as a conduit of grace to comfort the spirit, nurture hope, and represent the presence of a loving God within a multicultural, ecumenical environment. Joan ministers to pregnant women who are incarcerated by helping them work through their grief and anger at not being able to raise their newborns. She acts as their labor buddy, chaplain and "mother" as they go through labor and delivery. To connect the world of the prison and the church, the congregation where Joan serves as minister of reconciliation sends pink or blue baby Bibles and letters of encouragement to the inmates and to the babies' caregivers. She also serves as a chaplain and spiritual director to adolescent girls in residential treatment facilities. Joan and her congregation provide a ministry of care with families who have experienced the loss of a baby within the first 20 weeks of pregnancy and she leads an annual memorial service at the church. Joan fulfills the ministry of the deacon by connecting the hurting needs in the world with the response of the church.

Reflection

- It has been said that the scope of ministry for deacons is determined by the needs in society. To know the needs one must prayerfully read the signs of the times. As you learn about the news, what are some of the signs in your community and in the world that reflect areas of ministry in which deacons might serve?
- How does the ministry of the deacon reflect servant ministry and servant leadership?
- Do you have gifts, talents and/or interests that reflect the specialized ministry of a deacon? What are some of them? Visit www.explorecalling.org to learn more about identifying your spiritual gifts.
- How might these special gifts, talents or interests be used as a deacon on behalf of the church in the service of Christ's mission and ministry?

The Pastoral Ministry of Elders and Local Pastors

The United Methodist Church ordains as elders those whose leadership includes preaching and teaching, administering the sacraments, and leading the church in mission and service. Additionally, those appointed to perform the duties of a pastor but are not ordained, have a license for pastoral ministry.

In The United Methodist Church, a pastoral charge consists of one or more local churches or congregations to which an ordained or licensed pastor is appointed as lead pastor. In larger churches there may be additional ordained elders or licensed personnel appointed as associates. In some communities of faith, the pastor in charge may participate in a team ministry that includes local pastors, associate members, deacons, and laity. In other instances, two pastors may be appointed as co-pastors of a church or charge. Sometimes several local churches form a cooperative parish, group ministry, or extended parish that has a staff including more than one ordained minister and other paid staff persons. The paid church staff of larger churches or cooperative parishes may include administrators, educators, music and age group specialists, and others who provide services to congregation and community. Some of these persons may be diaconal ministers; others may be mission personnel of the General Board of Global Ministries.

Whether the parish is large or small, the tasks of the licensed or ordained minister who is a pastor are similar. The responsibilities of a pastor include the ministry of Word, Service, Sacrament, and Order and are outlined below.

In the context of this fourfold ministry, a pastor gives attention to the following duties:

1. Word and ecclesial acts
- preaching the Word of God and teaching the scriptures
- personal, ethical, and spiritual counseling
- performing weddings and funerals
- visiting the community of faith, the sick, aged, imprisoned, and others in need
- maintaining all confidences within the limits of the law

2. Sacrament
- administering the sacraments of baptism and Holy Communion
- encouraging the private and congregational use of other means of grace

3. Order
- being the administrative officer of the local church
- administering the day-to-day business of the church
- participating in denominational and conference programs
- leading the congregation in racial and ethnic inclusiveness

4. Service
- embodying the ministry of Jesus in servant ministries and servant leadership
- giving leadership in ordering the congregation for ministry in the world
- building the body of Christ as a caring and giving community
- participating in community, ecumenical, and interreligious concerns

Pastors vary widely in their interests, skills, and attitudes. These characteristics, combined with the needs of the parish, lead pastors to devote quite different proportions of time to the major tasks described above. Though the pastors of large churches may specialize in one or two of these basic areas of responsibility, most pastors must attend to all of the duties while, at the same time, caring for their own personal needs and the needs of their families. The following stories give insight into ways these duties are lived out in a variety of settings.

A Journal of Pastoral Ministries

Sunday: Sunyoung is a recent seminary graduate appointed as an associate pastor of a large suburban church. She was up earlier than usual this morning because it was one of the few Sundays of the year that she would preach at the 8:30 a.m. and 11:00 a.m. worship services. Normally, her participation in worship is limited to the reading of scripture or a prayer. Though preaching, she still led a young adult class during the Sunday school hour and met with the youth in the evening. At the end of this busy day, Tim, a leader in the youth group, wanted to discuss how to help a friend with a problem.

⏤⏤

Monday: A clergy couple, Doug and Sandy, are assigned to a rural circuit. After breakfast, they worked on the worship plans for the coming Sunday and reviewed their busy schedule for the week. While Sandy read some background material for her sermon, Doug prepared a column for the church newsletter. Their work together was cut short when Sue came by to ask Doug's help in finding a convalescent home for her 86-year-old mother. After lunch, Sandy visited several members in the hospital, while Doug contacted the director of a United Methodist home to find out what options were open to Sue and her mother. After dinner, Doug had a meeting at church, while Sandy relaxed after a busy day.

Elders have the primary responsibility for administering the sacraments of baptism and Holy Communion. Bishop Jim Dorff, center, blesses the Communion bread, assisted by the Rev. Forbes Matonga, an elder, and the Rev. Kim Ingram, a deacon.

Tuesday: Rod is the pastor of a growing urban African American congregation. Early in the morning, he was out of the parsonage sitting on the bench at the bus stop talking with people as they left for work. By discovering who they were and what they did, he had an opportunity to do some street counseling and introduce them to the ministry of the church. By 8 a.m., he was at the hospital with the Jacksons during Mr. Jackson's surgery. The family had a lot of questions about hospital procedures, death, and faith. This was his first opportunity to become better acquainted with this family. He returned to the church office about 10:30 a.m. and completed plans for the Sunday service. Rod had lunch with a committee working on ways to get tutoring services for children who are not sufficiently served by the existing public school programs. Later in the day, he saw a man who needed help getting a job, a couple who are going through divorce, and a teenager who thinks she is pregnant.

Wednesday: Juanita is a local pastor of a small Hispanic congregation trying to establish itself in a satellite city of a major metropolitan area. The Spanish language population of the city has grown rapidly as new residents have settled into this relatively small urban area. In the middle of the morning, Juanita met with the personnel manager of a local factory to see if there were any jobs open for the unemployed of her community. In the afternoon, she walked through the neighborhood talking with the people she saw. She uncovered more needs than she could ever hope to address. She was joined by her lay leader that evening, and together they sat down with the board of trustees of the church which allows them to share facilities. There is frustration over the additional maintenance costs of housing two congregations in the same building. Juanita yearns for the day when her congregation can have a church building of its own.

Thursday: Linda is the pastor of a small-town church. After getting her youngest child off to school, she headed for a meeting with the other pastors of the district. They discussed special offerings and plans for a lay leadership training program and then were addressed by an interdenominational panel of clergy on the ecumenical concerns of the area. During lunch, Linda received word that Mr. Young had died and the funeral would be on Saturday afternoon. She left the luncheon early and went directly to the Young residence. Sandra Young and the children were upset and needed Linda's support and prayers, so she stayed with them the rest of the afternoon. After dinner with her family, she met with the team of visitors who would go to the homes of new residents, visitors to the church, the sick, and the bereaved. Their awareness of Mr. Young's death made them more sensitive to the importance of their tasks.

Elders can also serve outside the local church. The Rev. Dr. Kah-Jin Jeffrey Kuan, an elder, is president of Claremont School of Theology.

Friday: George is an ordained elder on a parish ministry team. Since Friday is his day off he finished preparing for worship on Thursday afternoon before meeting with the parish ministry team. He plans to spend his day running errands for home, exercising, and going out with friends for dinner. He will meet on Saturday with other church leaders to reflect on the current ministries of the church and plan for the upcoming month. He did receive a couple phone calls from church members, but since it was his day off he scheduled meetings with them for the following week.

Saturday: Minsuk is a Korean pastor who is working hard to develop a small congregation in a metropolitan area. He was up early, as usual, and began the day in prayer with his family. They prayed for one another, the church, the needs of its members, and the world. After breakfast Minsuk read a little, reworked a section of his sermon, and made copies of the Sunday bulletin. He then spent a few hours calling on church members before returning to the church for an afternoon youth meeting. Soon after the youth left the church, a young couple arrived with their friends and family to rehearse a wedding which would take place on Sunday afternoon. After a rehearsal dinner, Paul had time to spend with his preschooler before he put her to bed. Minsuk and his wife have adapted to their work schedules by looking to the middle of the week for the family time they often miss on weekends.

Reflection

- How does the ministry of a pastor with its multiple responsibilities and opportunities relate to the gifts you might bring to this ministry? Can you see yourself fitting in a multi-functional lifestyle of a pastor?
- How is pastoral ministry complimentary to lay ministry within the local church?

Chaplaincy and Pastoral Counseling

If you did not already know, you have discovered by reading this book that United Methodist clergy can serve God's people in places other than United Methodist congregations. Did you know that deacons, elders, and local pastors can also serve as pastoral counselors or chaplains?

Deacons, elders, and local pastors can serve in ministries of pastoral care in specialized settings. Deacons, elders, associate members, and provisional members may be endorsed after completing the requirements. Local pastors may be granted associate status by the United Methodist Endorsing Agency.

A primary difference between these appointments and the local church is the nature of the institution in which ministry takes place and the role of the clergy in that institution. Some of the institutions where chaplains serve include hospitals, hospice, prisons, industry, the workplace, and the military services. Pastoral counselors are found in private practice as well as on the staff of pastoral counseling centers.

Many times, chaplains and pastoral counselors serve institutions that are culturally diverse and multidisciplinary. While chaplains perform traditional functions such as rites, sacraments, ordinances, pastoral care and religious education, they also perform nontraditional roles that vary based on the needs of their ministry setting

Descriptions of Chaplains and Pastoral Counselors

Hospital Chaplains

Every day, hospital chaplains help patients and their relatives cope with sickness, disability, and even death. In mental hospitals, the problems are perhaps even more excruciating. Chaplains in these settings are part of a team. They work shoulder to shoulder with doctors, nurses, psychiatrists, and social workers.

The role of the chaplain is to provide pastoral care for patients, their families, and for staff. They reach out to those on the wards and in the surgery and critical care waiting rooms. Generally, they will be on ethics committees as the hospital considers complex issues of modern

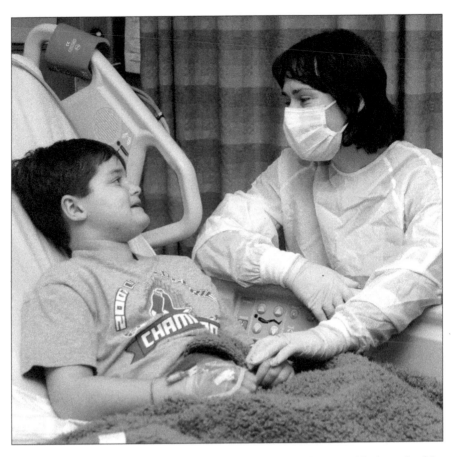

Workplace and military chaplains provide counseling and pastoral care outside the walls of the traditional church in settings such as hospitals, prisons, and the armed forces.

medicine. They frequently lead Bible studies and conduct worship services in hospital chapels.

Prison Chaplains

"I was in prison and you visited me" (Matthew 25:36). In the correctional setting (prisons, jails, detention facilities), chaplains have the opportunity to pastor unique and diverse communities, in both traditional and nontraditional ways. They preach, teach, baptize, serve Holy Communion, counsel, visit, and serve the prisoner congregation. They are pastors not only to inmates, but also to the staff and the families of both communities. They serve and are available to all the people incarcerated in their institution, providing for spiritual needs regardless of religious affiliation. This involves recruiting, training, and supervising a broad variety of religious volunteers from surrounding communities. They serve as a link between the religious communities on the outside and those on the inside, helping to build bridges of care and service both ways.

Industry/Workplace Chaplains

The success of industry is typically measured by the rate of production and flow of profit. The industrial chaplain stands in the middle of the needs of management and those of the men and women who power the industrial machine. When workers arrive on the job, they bring with them everything that is going on in their lives — from the joy of a newborn baby to a nagging problem with alcohol — and inevitably it affects their job performance.

Chaplains provide a ministry to people in business and industry, responding to individual and family needs as well as work life concerns such as job stress and career. They provide a preventative, as well as a problem-solving ministry, that reaches out with a concern for all people.

Chaplains work with industrial management at a number of levels. They frequently train supervisors on the line to relate more effectively to their workers who appear to be suffering from a personal problem. The chaplain is also influential at the policy level, conferring with management when new policies are proposed. Individual counseling often leads to referrals to in-house programs or community social services.

Military Chaplains

The role of the military chaplain is not to justify war, but to minister to the spiritual needs of service men and women and their families in a unique setting. Military chaplains are never asked to violate the tenets of their own faith as they work in a pluralistic arena in both war and peace. The chaplain trains with the service members and prepares to be spiritually, mentally, and physically ready to go wherever and whenever service members are deployed world-wide.

The chaplain serves on the staff of the commander and has ready access to service members on flight lines, in motor pools, on ships, and in the field environment. On military installations and bases, worship services are conducted in beautifully appointed chapels with ongoing weekday ministries in the chapels or family life centers. The United Methodist Church endorses chaplains for full-time, active duty, as well as for reserve component duty, concurrent with local church or other specialized ministry.

Pastoral Counselors

While it is true that all pastors counsel people, pastoral counselors endorsed by the United Methodist Endorsing Agency have undergone additional specialized training so they can integrate resources of scripture and faith with insights from the behavioral sciences. Pastoral counselors serve on staffs of local churches, in pastoral counseling centers, in health care institutions, or in private practice.

The Uniqueness of Ministry Endorsed by the United Methodist Endorsing Agency

Clergy endorsed by the United Methodist Endorsing Agency operate in culturally and religiously diverse settings. They serve people who may or may not be United Methodists. Yet strangely, there is identification with the chaplain or pastoral counselor if he or she is credible and relevant to the needs of the individual within that institution.

Many times, the ministry takes place with clergy from other faith groups such as Roman Catholic, Jewish, Muslim, Orthodox, or other Protestants. Each chaplain is required to provide religious support which consists of rites, sacraments, ordinances, pastoral care, and religious education within their faith group, or to coordinate for someone else to accommodate a belief system that conflicts with their own.

Chaplains are expected to be both pastoral and prophetic to the institution. Sometimes, chaplains are required to advise the institutional leadership on ethics and the impact of decisions on people.

Unlike the local church, coordinating resources for ministry is done within the administrative processes of another institution. The coordination may require securing a place for religious activities, funds, and other resources such as transportation, supplies, equipment, and even permission for people to be free to attend certain events.

- Do you sense a call to chaplaincy or pastoral counseling? What type of ministry interests you?
- What specific gifts, training, education, and work experience do you bring to the unique requirement of this specialized ministry?
- Are you flexible enough to accommodate religious pluralism and work within distinctively diverse cultures/organizational systems?

Higher Education Collegiate Ministry

Settings and Personnel

The United Methodist Church is in ministry on many college and university campuses in the U.S. These represent many kinds of ministry settings.

- Some are Wesley Foundations or Wesley Fellowships (United Methodist Collegiate Ministry sites funded in large part by annual conference budgets).
- Others are ecumenical ministries (cooperating in the name of United Methodism with one or more denominations that share funding responsibilities).
- Some collegiate ministries are staffed by chaplains at United Methodist-related or other private universities and colleges (these are funded by the school itself).
- Some are ministries established by one or more local congregations. They may meet at a local church or elsewhere near campus. They may be staffed by campus ministers who also serve a congregation.

At independent or church-related colleges and universities, the chaplain may be part of the student affairs office or the religion department. Or, the chaplain may report directly to the president's office. Church-related institutions usually provide on campus space for the chaplain's office and activities.

At some private colleges and universities, there may be a chaplain and a United Methodist campus minister. While the chaplain is responsible for the entire campus community (which may include interfaith relations and programming), the United Methodist campus minister's primary responsibility is to serve the Wesley Foundation or Fellowship on campus.

At public colleges and universities, the campus ministry may be located adjacent to the campus in a church owned building, although schools sometime provide space on campus. Campus ministers at commuter and community colleges may not be campus based at all, but work out of local churches or other offices. They do much of their ministry in the context of the community college's own cycle of activities.

Some campus ministers and chaplains are ordained elders or deacons; others are not. There are also deaconesses, home missioners, US-2 and mission interns who serve as campus ministers.

Some work fulltime on campus; others are part-time. Campus ministers who are ordained are employed by a college, university, ecumenical agency, or local church and are appointed by and accountable to the bishop of their annual conference. Of the many colleges and universities served by The United Methodist Church, the campuses and student bodies vary dramatically.

- One campus minister develops programs on a small residential campus where students are quite accessible, since they live and work on campus.
- Another works on a large, urban, commuter campus where students spend little time on the campus, either before or after classes.
- Still another may serve a sprawling university campus where students of all ages have a variety of lifestyles and live in a variety of situations, both on campus and off.
- A chaplain may work on a large private university campus where students, faculty and staff represent multiple faith traditions.
- Another may work on a smaller United Methodist-related college campus where a majority of the students are Christian.

The Ministry on the Campus

For all these settings, ministry with students is a central emphasis. But campus ministers and chaplains are also concerned with faculty, staff, and administrators. As the name implies, collegiate ministry is a ministry to the whole campus, and encompasses many models for relating to everyone affiliated with college and university campuses.

Collegiate ministry could be 200 people gathered for a weekend conference examining sexuality from sociological, psychological, and theological perspectives. It could mean a lively discussion about religion and the arts, or about religion and the anatomy lab. Collegiate ministry could be a small group of students gathered late on a weeknight for prayer and Holy Communion at a nearby United Methodist church.

Here are other examples of how collegiate ministers are engaged in ministry:

She's a first semester student, new to the campus. She is isolated, lost, and agonizing over whether to quit and go home. She's asking for emotional support, but she also wants spiritual guidance. The campus minister has a working relationship with the campus counseling center. They work together to serve the whole student in providing the support she needs.

He is a senior who still hasn't declared a major. He knows he's in trouble. But he's labored so long under his parents' expectations, his professors' expectations and the expectations of his peers that he feels paralyzed, unable to make up his mind. The campus minister, who also serves at a local church, connects the student to a member of the congregation who works in the field about which the student is truly passionate.

Students from the Wesley Foundation at Florida International University/Miami-Dade College during a retreat at Fort Myers, Fla. The theme was "Overcome."

The professor stops by again today, "just to talk." His wife died suddenly last semester, and he wonders how he can keep getting up every morning and going to class. The campus minister knows that the professor considers himself to be "spiritual but not religious" and listens with compassion.

There has been racial tension on the campus for a week. On Friday, the university president called asking for support in addressing the issue. The university chaplain gathers the campus ministers, who represent various faith groups, to formulate a plan of how they can diffuse the tension and nurture a stronger sense of community.

Creationism. Intelligent design. Evolution. The discussion at the university is generating lots of heat but little common ground. The vice president for academic affairs and the chair of the biosciences department decide to ask if the university chaplain would take a hand in sponsoring a campus-wide forum to focus the debate. The chaplain pulls together a panel of experts from the university and the wider community to participate in the forum.

Ministry in higher education is demanding. It's also rewarding. Being a campus minister or a university chaplain demands a diversity of gifts, skills, education, commitments, and roles: preacher, teacher, negotiator, spiritual counselor, pastor, official college representative, public worship leader, small group convener, support for parents, adviser to university professors and administrators. It can be fast-paced, stressful, and demanding. But it is also stimulating, challenging, and deeply rewarding.

Campus ministers and university chaplains work with people ranging from 18-year-old high school graduates to senior adult faculty members and students. The campus minister's "congregation" may be racial-ethnic students and staff; second career and returning women undergrads; science, law, and medical school students; students who are single parents; veterans returning to school after their military service; members of fraternities and sororities or the custodial and maintenance staff.

Collegiate Ministry Issues and Opportunities

In addition to caring for people, those who minister in higher education also care about issues of values and education; what it means to be an educated person and a Christian; how faith and knowledge contribute to educating people to be contributing citizens of society and of the world. All of these are important facets of the work of a collegiate minister in higher education.

Some campus ministers and chaplains teach courses in religion and other disciplines; some teach courses for credit in the curriculum, while others teach noncredit courses. Those who teach for credit often have completed, in addition to their theological degree, a doctorate (Ph.D., Ed.D., Th.D.) in the academic area.

Some teach in departments other than religion, such as philosophy, psychology, sociology, English, economics, or other areas. This means the individual is employed as a faculty member and meets the same academic preparation requirements as other faculty. The annual conference may appoint an ordained clergyperson to teach at the institution. And elders, deacons, or lay people may serve in administrative positions in the college or university, such as counselor, dean, or president.

Ministry in higher education engages mind and heart. It engages students and staff, faculty and administrators, the church and the world. It engages knowledge and vital piety. Writer Madeleine L'Engle sums up her experience in higher education in this way: "My own college years were a mixture of joy and pain."[3] Joy and pain. And the minister is there for all of it. That is why collegiate ministry is so important, so challenging, and so unpredictable. It is a valid and valued calling.

Reflection

- Think about unique gifts you may have to relate to young people who are making vocational decisions about their future.
- How may you be uniquely suited, or not, to work with college students, faculty and staff of all ages to help them grow in their faith development?
- How comfortable are you in relating to people of all faiths, or those who profess no faith, in an academic environment?
- Visit www.explorecalling.org to learn more about identifying your spiritual gifts.

Mission Personnel

God calls all Christians to be in mission. Some are called to a particular mission witness and service through channels of ministry provided by the church.

General Board of Global Ministries

The United Methodist General Board of Global Ministries is authorized to recruit, send, and receive missionaries, enabling them to dedicate all or a portion of their lives in service across cultural, national, and political boundaries . . . and to facilitate the receiving and assignment of missionaries . . .in cooperation with the other general agencies and with annual conferences (*Book of Discipline*).

Other responsibilities of Global Ministries are numerous. A long list of duties can be summarized around four goals:

- To make disciples of Jesus Christ.
- To grow and strengthen congregations and their communities.
- To alleviate human suffering.
- To promote justice, peace, and freedom.

Missionary Services

Global Ministries Missionary Services deals specifically with the identification, recruitment, selection, preparation, training, assignment, supervision, and support of mission personnel. It works with other units of the board in making decisions about personnel placements and assignments. Whenever possible, the placement of mission personnel is done in cooperation with United Methodist or other partner churches in the area of assignment.

The specific responsibilities of the Missionary Services office are:

- To promote the opportunities for mission service related to Global Ministries throughout the constituencies of the church.

Deaconess Cindy Johnson (left) and Brownsville, Texas, resident Antonia Redonda organize to stop construction of a border wall along the U.S.-Mexico border. Immigrant rights is one of many social justice concerns engaged by deaconess and home missioner ministries.

- To recruit, select, prepare, and assign mission personnel, including, but not limited to, missionaries, Generation Transformation Global Mission Fellows, Church and Community Workers, and National Plan for Hispanic/Latino Ministries missionaries.
- To provide all mission personnel with preparation and training for effective service in Global ministries.
- To evaluate mission personnel for appropriate placement.
- To recommend persons as candidates for commissioning as missionaries, and to supervise and confirm the completion of all requirements for commissioning.
- To engage in supervision and support of mission personnel through referral, transfer procedures, career counseling, missionary wellness, and personnel development, assisting them in the fulfillment of their missional vocation.
- To administer a diverse program of remuneration and benefits for personnel service.
- To offer training for mission service throughout the global church.
- To work with ecumenical agencies in fulfilling mission personnel responsibilities.
- To facilitate the receiving and assigning of missionaries — laity and clergy — from central conferences [outside the U.S.] and from autonomous, affiliated autonomous, and united churches, in cooperation with other boards and agencies and with annual conferences.
- To foster the support of mission personnel by congregations and individuals through Covenant Relationship Program, a feature of The Advance for Christ and His Church and expand other forms of mission commitment including Global Mission Partners.

Mission Service Types and Categories

There are three primary types of relationships between mission personnel and the General Board of Global Ministries.

- Commissioned personnel are missionaries, and others with whom the church has established a covenant involving the "laying on of hands" for mission service.

- Non-commissioned personnel have not entered into a covenant but serve in a variety of capacities and locations.
- Nationals in Mission are mission personnel of Central Conferences and partner churches outside the United States that the board helps to support.

Commissioned Personnel

Missionaries

International Service
Many missionaries are called to serve outside their country of origin, as pastors, teachers, doctors, nurses (or in other healing ministries), social workers, church planters, evangelists, and in a variety of other ways through various forms of denominational or ecumenical ministries. They engage in work relating to leadership development; ministry with the poor; global health; and new church starts. Global Ministries missionaries typically serve three-year, renewable terms. The majority of assignments are outside of the United States.

U.S. Service

National Plan for Hispanic Latino Ministry Missionaries
Responding to the General Conference decision to implement a National for Hispanic Latino Ministry (NPHLM), Global Ministries created the category of the NPHLM missionaries. This plan incorporates the missionaries as resources to implement the plan's overall strategy in the annual conferences. Thus assignments are made in partnership with annual conferences and these missionaries have the goal of reaching the growing Hispanic Latino population in the United States through the implementation of the National Plan for Hispanic Latino Ministry.

Church and Community Workers
The Church and Community Worker movement emerged more than a century ago to provide service and leadership development ministries in isolated rural areas. Today church and community workers work to uplift the poor and disenfranchised in rural and urban areas,

primarily in the United States. Workers are assigned to cooperative parishes, ethnic ministries, criminal justice ministries, congregational health ministries, cooperative ministries, mission institutions, immigration services, and rural and urban ministries. Some are deaconesses or home missioners. Both clergy and laity may serve in this mission category.

Young Adult Missionaries

Generation Transformation
Global Mission Fellows program is a leadership development and mission service opportunity that allows young adults age 20 through 30 to take part in mission and social justice ministries in both international and domestic contexts. It encourages participants to live out the transforming gospel of Jesus Christ by engaging with and learning from communities that are working for personal and social holiness and systemic change. The program builds upon Global Ministries' historic US-2 and Mission Intern programs, and is now open to young adults outside of the United States to participate in mission service abroad and in their own home country.

Global Mission Fellows serving internationally participate in a 25-month cycle of service—approximately 23 months internationally followed by two months of integrating their international experiential learning into their domestic setting.

Global Mission Fellows serving within their home country engage in mission service for two years with United Methodist partner organizations. Fellows serving in their own country explore their ministry and its relationship within the larger national and global context of mission. This will be available to those in the U.S., through a revised version of the US-2 program. Other domestic service opportunities are being developed in other countries.

Non-Commissioned Personnel

The category of non-commissioned personnel covers groups and people with ties to the General Board of Global Ministries, but who are not in covenant relationships. They may be engaged in time-limited projects or provide support services. One group, community developers, operate from local bases but form a network that the board services.

Mission Volunteers are not considered mission personnel, and the church provides no compensation or benefits for them. The United Methodist Church and its annual conferences in the U.S. offer a wide variety of volunteer mission opportunities for both teams and individuals and volunteers perform extremely valuable mission service. Every annual conference has a Volunteer In Mission coordinator and the annual conferences work cooperatively with the General Board of Global Ministries through the Mission Volunteers program area.

Nationals in Mission are mission personnel from partner churches outside the United States, serving in their own or another country. They serve in a variety of positions involving education, health care, leadership training.

Reflection

- Through Global Ministries, lay or ordained people (beginning as young adults) can respond to the call to mission service, in short-term service or lifetime commitment; in many different positions; and in many different locations. How would you describe this call as different from every Christian's call to servant ministry?
- What gifts, skills, and interests could you bring to any of the multiple ways that one might be in mission service on behalf of the church either nationally or internationally?

Notes

1. The Rev. Dr. Martin Luther King Jr, "The Drum Major Instinct" (sermon delivered at Ebenezer Baptist Church, Atlanta, Ga., February 1968).
2. Summarized from *The Book of Discipline* of The United Methodist Church (Nashville: The United Methodist Publishing House), p. 221, 246.
3. Madeline L'Engle, *Two-Part Invention: The Story of a Marriage* (San Francisco: Harper & Row, 1988).

Chapter Three
Steps Into Servant Leadership

Steps Into Ministry for Young People

Maybe you are exploring how God wants you to live your life. You may be beginning to think about vocational choices; or you may be experiencing a strong inclination toward a particular occupation or profession. You read in Chapter One that coming to a place where God's intention for you and your gifts and talents match is a powerful indication of God's vocational call to you. Perhaps you do not feel any special calling, particularly to ordained ministry. However, you may be wondering what it might mean for you to respond as a baptized Christian to servant ministry.

The question is not whether you are called. The question is: How is God calling you to serve?

Those answering a call to licensed or ordained ministry are considered clergy. Servant leadership of other Christians is considered ministry of the laity.

Whether your vocation and career choice leads you to serve in lay or ordained ministry, listen to God's voice, seek wise counsel, do your own study and reflection, and follow the direction in which you are led.

Vicki Brown/GBHEM

- Talk with your youth minister, your church pastor or other church leader, your campus minister or chaplain.
- Meet with a peer group and adults you respect who are engaged in a type of ministry that interests you.
- Seek honest feedback from people who know you well and can help you identify your gifts and talents.
- Read and reflect about the categories of service in this book.

Bishop Robert Hayes Jr. prays with a young man during a commitment service at Exploration 2011.

- Explore different websites such as www.explorecalling.org and www.gbhem.org/candidacy to find out about more about Christian vocation, how to answer God's call in your life, and identifying your spiritual gifts.
- Above all, talk to God, listen to God, and wait for and respond to God's direction.

Opportunities for Young People for Servant Leadership

- If you feel called into ordained ministry, talk with your pastor or other clergy person about steps to exploring this call (see pp. 76-78 for Steps into Ordained Ministry).
- If you feel called to serve in ministry with young people, there are opportunities, such as internships and shadow programs that give you a chance to learn from others in children's, youth, campus ministry, or missions. Talk with church leaders to see if

these opportunities are available at your church.

- Churches often sponsor regional camps that hire college-age students to be on the ministry staff during the summer. Often these camps need counselors-in-training, as well, and hire older high school students for these positions. Contact your region's youth or camping ministry director to learn more.

Consider the following as you make a vocational choice:

Your Gifts — What spiritual gifts do you have to offer the church? What do you do well? What do you enjoy? If you enjoy writing, offer to write a prayer for the congregation. If you are friendly and enjoy meeting people, offer to serve as a church greeter. If you are a good leader, volunteer to be an officer for your youth or college group. If you like to make speeches, consider training to become an official lay speaker. You may want to consider asking your pastor about gifts discovery inventories to help you identify what your gifts are. Whatever your gifts, discover ways the church can use them, or visit www.explorecalling.org for more information.

Your Passion — What really motivates you? Maybe you see a homeless person and want to make a change. Maybe you read about genocide in foreign countries and want to help stop it. Or maybe you're tired of hearing about young people being bullied and hurting each other. How is the church responding? What ways could the church respond? How might you get involved or lead the movement yourself? Social justice ministries are important to the life of the church.

Your Daily Living — Think of ways you can incorporate what you know and learn from your faith into your daily living. You know you are empowered to live as Jesus lived. What does that mean in how you treat your friends and peers? How does that shape your response to your family? Remember that the way you live is a ministry in itself.

Your Career Path — Have you already started thinking about your profession? As you choose your career, think of ways you can serve God in what you do. You may want to consider a career in the church. Churches sometimes need teachers for church schools. Conferences usually have communicators who write for newspapers, oversee website development, and work with the media. Some congregations have parish nurses, and many churches hire business administrators to oversee the finances and business end of running a church. Think about how to shape your career as a service for God.

Your Devotional Life — Whatever ministry role you take, you must be prepared and fit for leadership. Taking Bible study courses and/or carving daily time for reading Scripture (even if just for five minutes) will better prepare you for your ministry.

Your Prayers — Be steadfast in prayer about what ways God can use you. Ask for guidance from God and be still to listen for God's

Mike DuBose/UM News Service

Once you are certain you want to attend seminary, investigate United Methodist Loans and Scholarships at www.gbhem.org/loansandscholarships. The Rev. Glenn "Chebon" Kernell received scholarships supported by Native American Ministries Sunday.

direction. Ask others to pray for you as you discern what leadership you will take as a minister.

Steps Into Laity Leadership

The leadership of the laity has a long history in The United Methodist Church. While Methodist pastors rode the circuits, it was the leadership of the lay members of the societies that kept the congregational ministry going.

Beginning Steps

A good beginning step, if you feel you may be experiencing a call to serve, is to complete a spiritual gifts inventory. Study and reflect upon how your gifts, talents, and strengths, may be used in ministry, and/or in your daily life, community, and church. Take some time to consider your passion. What inspires you? What areas of mission or ministry excite you? What issues in the church or community bring you the deepest concern? When you use your spiritual gifts in conjunction with an area of ministry that you are passionate about wonderful things can and do happen.

Another step is critically important as you explore and prepare yourself for any form of ministry. Remain steadfast in the basic Christian practices or spiritual disciplines which John Wesley called means of grace. These means of grace include prayer, Bible study, the sacrament of Holy Communion, worship, fasting, and Christian conferencing. You may join or form a small group that will help you grow spiritually and stay faithful in your spiritual practices.

One group of this kind is a Covenant Discipleship Group. Small groups for support and accountability are a rich part of our Wesleyan heritage and continue today in many churches with a renewed vitality and relevance for growing in discipleship. Today's Covenant Discipleship Groups help their members witness to Jesus Christ in the world and follow his teachings through acts of compassion, justice, worship, and devotion under the guidance of the Holy Spirit. They focus on a balanced discipleship through works of piety (personal devotions and public worship) and works of mercy (acts of compassion and acts of justice).

Steps to Get Started with a Covenant Discipleship Group

- For your reading:
  - > *Accountable Discipleship: Living in God's Household*, Steven W. Manskar, Discipleship Resources
  - > *Covenant Discipleship: Christian Formation Through Mutual Accountability*, David Lowes Watson, Wipf & Stock Publishers
- After reading the recommended books, meet with your pastor to discuss introducing Covenant Discipleship groups to the congregation. The step-by-step process is found in *Forming Christian Disciples: The Role of Covenant Discipleship* and *Class Leaders in the Congregation* by David Lowes Watson.
- If Covenant Discipleship groups are part of your congregational disciple formation process, tell your pastor that you want to join a group. If there is no room in existing groups, then form a new group.
- Go to www.gbod.org/covenantdiscipleship to find more information on Covenant Discipleship Groups.

Opportunities and Steps for Servant Leadership

Class Leaders

Class leaders led the laity of the early Methodist church in developing their discipleship. Today, class leaders may be commissioned and classes may be organized to help form faithful disciples of Jesus Christ.

Today, class leaders meet weekly with a Covenant Discipleship group and have been commissioned by the congregation in consultation with the pastor. A class leader is given pastoral responsibility for 15-20 members of the congregation who want to grow in their discipleship. The class does not meet. The class leader helps them grow in discipleship through regular visits, telephone conversations, email, social media, and post. Class leaders help members of their class grow in discipleship by practicing the General Rule of Discipleship: "To witness to Jesus Christ in the world and to follow his teaching through acts of compassion, justice, worship and devotion under the guidance of the Holy Spirit."

Class leaders join in partnership with the appointed pastor in the work of making disciples of Jesus Christ for the transformation of the world. The pastor meets monthly with the class leaders.

If you feel called to use your gifts in this way:

- Assess your spiritual gifts. The gifts of teaching and leadership are helpful for this ministry role.
- Study the role of class leader by reading ¶ 117.2.c, 2012 *Book of Discipline*.
- Read *Class Leaders: Recovering a Tradition*, David Lowes Watson, Discipleship Resources.

Ministry Area or Committee Chair

Leading within the congregation as part of a ministry team, committee member or committee chair is another form of servant ministry or servant leadership for lay people.

Resources to help you:

- Participate in a spiritual gifts study to determine your spiritual gifts or complete a spiritual gifts assessment.
- Share the results of your spiritual gifts assessment with your pastor and/or the chair of the Lay Leadership Committee.
- Read a copy of the *Guidelines for Leading Your Congregation*, available from Cokesbury, for the area or committee of interest to you.
- Make your interest known to the pastor or nominating committee in your congregation so your name may be considered in this way.

Lay Member to Annual Conference

Lay members to annual conference have the responsibility to represent their congregation at annual conference and help interpret the actions and activities of the annual conference to their congregations. To consider this servant leadership position:

- You must be a professing member of The United Methodist Church for two years and active in The United Methodist Church for four years.
- Lay members to annual conference are elected by the charge conference of your church.

Lay Leader

Lay leaders function as the primary representatives of the laity in the local church, district, or annual conference to which they are elected. The role of lay leader is not only to represent the laity, but also to support the pastor. In correlating positions, the district lay leader supports the district superintendent, while the conference lay leader supports the bishop. Laity in these roles can be prayer partners and share in mutual ministry with the clergy leaders.

Steps to take include:

- Assess your spiritual gifts. The gift of leadership is helpful for this role in the church.
- Lay leaders must be professing members of the local church and are elected by the charge conference of that church.
- Read the *Lay Leader/Lay Member Guidelines*, available from Cokesbury, to discover the responsibilities and considerations for the role of lay leader in the local church.
- It is a good option for lay leaders to consider becoming certified lay speakers.

Lay Servant

Exhorters in the early Methodist societies challenged and encouraged the members in their spiritual growth. After a sermon by the pastor an exhorter would give practical applications of the sermon to the society members. The term exhorter was eventually replaced by lay speaker. The role of lay speakers expanded well beyond pulpit supply into various types of leadership ministries and spiritual formation. In 2012 the General Conference approved legislation to change the name of this leadership development program to Lay Servant Ministries.

A lay servant is a professing member of a local church or charge who is ready and willing to serve the church and who is well informed on and committed to the Scriptures and the doctrine, heritage, organization, and life of The United Methodist Church and who has received specific training to develop skills in witnessing to the Christian faith through spoken communication, church and community leadership, and care-giving ministries.

Lay servants serve in their local church, or with additional training, serve beyond their local church in other churches, the district or the annual conference. Lay servant training is no longer focused on preaching. There are many more courses on other areas of ministry, mission, and spiritual formation.

Training to become a lay servant:

- Talk with your pastor regarding your interest in becoming a lay servant. Lay servants are recommended by their pastor and the church council or charge conference.
- Register for the Basic Course in Lay Servant Ministries at either the district or conference level. Your pastor can help you get in touch with your district office to find information on classes. A list of Conference Directors of Lay Servant Ministries may be found at www.gbod.org/laity under Lay Servant Ministries.
- The steps for becoming a certified lay speaker include:
  > Becoming a local church lay servant.
  > Taking an advanced Lay Servant Ministries course.
  > *The Book of Discipline* outlines the Lay Servant Ministries.

Lay Speaker

While the name of the overall leadership development program was changed from Lay Speaking Ministries to Lay Servant Ministries provisions were made for those who are gifted and called to provide pulpit supply.

A Lay Speaker is a certified lay servant who is called and equipped to serve the church in pulpit supply. Lay speakers must complete a specific list of courses provided in the Lay Servant Ministries Program. Lay speakers are certified by the annual conference after completion of the required courses, and examination with recommendation by the district committee on Lay Servant Ministries. Lay speakers must complete one advanced course and be re-examined and recommended by the district committee every three years to maintain their role as lay speakers.

Lay Missioner

Lay Missioners are committed lay persons, mostly volunteers, who are willing to be trained and work in a team with a pastor mentor to develop faith communities, establish community ministries, develop church school extension programs, and engage in congregational development. All lay missioners must follow the guidelines established by the National Committee on Hispanic Ministries of the National Plan for Hispanic Ministries and may be certified by their annual conference.

Lay missioners may be either Hispanic or non-Hispanic and must follow the guidelines found in the National Plan for Hispanic Ministry. Steps to become a lay missioner:

- Be an active participant in a local congregation of The United Methodist Church or the Methodist Church of Puerto Rico and demonstrate an appreciation for United Methodist doctrine and tradition as well as a knowledge of and commitment to the National Plan for Hispanic Ministries.
- Understand, appreciate, and affirm the existing Hispanic culture in the United States.
- Receive the recommendation of the pastor or appropriate committee of the local church in which you participate.
- Complete Modules I and II of the Training Program.

Certified Lay Minister

Since its inception, certified lay ministry has grown from providing pastoral leadership in small congregations to including service as an assistant to the pastor in larger churches, leading congregational care and health ministries, lay chaplaincy, starting house churches, partnering in new church planting efforts and other varied leadership positions within the church.

Go to www.gbod.org to find more information.

Steps to Become a Certified Lay Minister:

- Become a certified lay speaker or complete equivalent training.
- Study the guidelines for Certified Lay Ministry in the *Book of Discipline.*

- Study and demonstrate an appreciation for UM history, polity, doctrine, worship, and liturgy through service in your local church.
- Receive the recommendation of your pastor and voted approval of the church council or charge conference.
- Complete the courses recommended by the General Board of Discipleship and the General Board of Higher Education and Ministry.
- Submit to appropriate screening for ministry.
- Receive the recommendation of the district superintendent.
- Apply in writing to the district Committee on Ordained Ministry.
- Appear before the district Committee on Ordained Ministry for review and approval.

Certified Professional Lay Ministry

Lay people serving in the church can enhance their learning and increase their knowledge and skills to become more effective workers in their areas of service. Certification in various areas of ministry within the church is available. These include Christian education, youth ministry, music, evangelism, camp/retreat ministry, spiritual formation, and older adult ministry. See pages 85-86 for steps into certification for specialized ministry.

Leaders at any level set an example for others to follow. People will look to you as a leader, whether you are lay or clergy, for an example of how to live out their faith.

Commissioned Deaconess or Home Missioner

See pages 32-35 for more information about this lifetime, full-time mission-oriented service.

Reflection

- List some ways that you are providing servant leadership now? What are some ways you can improve?

Steps for Deaconess or Home Missioner

Deaconesses and home missioners are approved through a process established by United Methodist Women, consecrated and commissioned by a bishop at settings approved by the board of directors of United Methodist Women. They shall have a continuing relationship to the UMC through United Methodist Women. They are available for service with any agency or program of the UMC. Deaconesses and home missioners may also serve in church agencies or programs, provided that approval is given by United Methodist Women in consultation with the bishop in the receiving area.

Qualifications for the Office of Deaconess and Home Missioner
1. A call from God to lifetime, full-time mission-oriented service as part of the lay diaconate.
2. Membership in The United Methodist Church.
3. The professional training, education, and/or certifications for the ministry to which one is called.
4. At the time of consecration and commissioning, position (compensated or non-compensated) in an approved appointment of love, justice, and service. Appointments may be in a church-related vocation or helping profession. A deaconess or home missioner must hold local church membership in the annual conference in which she or he will be serving.
5. Continuation of the practice of discernment.
6. Biblical, theological, and sociological grounding in the prescribed core studies:
   a) Old Testament
   b) New Testament
   c) Theology of Mission
   d) History of The United Methodist Church
   e) Polity and Doctrine of the United Methodist Church

Core studies may be taken at United Methodist institutions of higher learning or at colleges, universities, and/or seminaries that are approved by the University Senate of The United Methodist Church. Intensive courses (one- to two-week) and other alternative program options are available. Prior coursework may be reviewed

74

for approval of the core studies. Limited financial assistance based on need is available for core study coursework.

7. Commitment to functioning through diverse forms of service directed toward the world to make Jesus Christ known in the fullness of his mission, which mandates that his followers:
   a) Alleviate suffering.
   b) Eradicate causes of injustice and all that robs life of dignity and worth.
   c) Facilitate the development of full human potential.
   d) Share in building global community through the church universal.

Application and Candidacy Process for Deaconess and Home Missioner

- Following a process of prayerful discernment that may include participation in a deaconess or home missioner spiritual formation retreat, the inquirer completes the application for deaconess or home missioner. This form is available online through the United Methodist Women website or through the administrative staff of the Office of Deaconess and Home Missioner.
- The application is processed by the Office of Deaconess and Home Missioner for distribution to a review committee and shared for recommendation with the appropriate conference committee for mission service.
- Upon the recommendation of the review committee, the applicant is invited for staff interview and psychological interview and testing and participation in the Theology of Mission course. The applicant must be interviewed within two years of the first invitation.
- If approved, the applicant moves to the candidacy stage, is matched with a mentor/coach and completes core studies with progress reviewed annually.
- Upon completion or near completion of core studies, the candidate is invited to participate in the next scheduled preparation and training for consecration and commissioning.
- A review of appointment is submitted by the Office of Deaconess and Home Missioner to the appointing bishop for approval.
- Upon completion of all requirements and approval of appoint-

ment, the candidate is consecrated to the Office of Deaconess and Home Missioner and commissioned by a bishop at settings approved by the board of directors of United Methodist Women. Deaconesses and home missioners have a continuing relationship to the UMC through United Methodist Women.

- The approved appointment is fixed by the appointing bishop.

Steps Into Licensed and Ordained Ministry

Candidacy for ordained ministry is the first set of formal steps through which a person moves toward ordination and annual conference membership as an ordained deacon or elder. If you would like to learn more about candidacy or begin the candidacy process for ordained ministry, talk with your pastor or another church leader who can help you explore the next steps for ministry.

A Master of Divinity degree from a University Senate-approved seminary is a requirement for ordination as an elder in The United Methodist Church. These graduates are from United Theological Seminary, one of the 13 UM seminaries.

The steps for the candidacy process are established by the General Conference and may vary some as changes and updates are made every four years. Steps may also vary depending on the requirements of the annual conference where the candidate applies. A detailed listing of the steps into ministry along with flyers you can download or print for more information is posted at www.gbhem.org/candidacy.

Whether you feel called to serve as a local pastor, a deacon or an elder, all those serving in licensed or ordained ministry must first enroll in and complete the process for certified candidacy.

Generally, the steps into licensed and ordained ministry include:

Candidacy

- Contact the church pastor or other clergy to inquire about the candidacy process.
- Be a member of the UMC or active, baptized participant in a United Methodist ministry setting for at least one year.
- Read *The Christian as Minister* and other resources as identified by your annual conference.
- Apply to the district superintendent in writing to be admitted to the candidacy process and assigned a candidacy mentor. Enroll in the online candidacy application system.
- Receive approval from the Staff/Pastor-Parish Relations Committee and the Charge Conference to proceed as a candidate.
- Complete psychological assessment and other background checks.
- Meet with the district Committee on Ordained Ministry to receive approval of certification for licensed or ordained ministry.
- To serve in licensed ministry as a local pastor, complete the requirements needed in order to receive approval for the license as pastoral ministry.
- Meet with the district Committee on Ordained Ministry annually to renew candidacy certification or approval of the license for pastoral ministry.

Associate Membership

- Associate members serve under the authority of a license that does not require annual renewal. They have an ongoing relationship with the annual conference that lasts into retirement.
- Local pastors must have reached a minimum of 40 years of age and four years of full-time service as a local pastor before applying for associate membership.
- Complete the requirements for associate membership as listed in *The Book of Discipline* and apply through the Board of Ordained Ministry to receive a recommendation for approval as an associate member.
- For more information, visit www.gbhem.org/localpastors.

Provisional Membership

- Complete educational requirements including undergraduate and graduate education.
- Complete a theological examination and present acceptable background checks and medical examination.
- Interview with the Board of Ordained Ministry and receive a recommendation to the clergy session for provisional membership.

Ordination as a Deacon or Elder

- Complete a minimum of two years (and no more than eight years) of provisional membership.
- Serve for a minimum of two years under full-time appointment while a provisional member.
- Meet requirements for provisional membership as established by the annual conference Board of Ordained Ministry; interview with the BOM to receive a recommendation to the clergy session for ordination and full membership.

Steps to Become Endorsed

Endorsement is the credential which certifies that a clergyperson performs a valid ministry of The United Methodist Church and has presented evidence of required specialized education, training, skills and, when required, professional certification necessary to perform that ministry. Once that clergyperson no longer serves in that particular setting, the endorsement is withdrawn.

Who Needs Endorsement?

The Book of Discipline states that the United Methodist Endorsing Agency has responsibility for people appointed to ministries of pastoral care in specialized settings including, but not limited to, ministry in the military, correctional institutions, the Department of Veterans Affairs, healthcare settings, pastoral counseling, marriage and family counseling, workplace ministries, community service ministries, life coach and other related ministry settings that conference Boards of Ordained Ministry and bishops may designate. Clergy to be appointed to any of the above extension ministry appointments shall receive ecclesiastical endorsement.

What is Endorsement and Ecclesiastical Approval?

Endorsement is the process established by the church to ensure clergy possess the skills, capabilities, and are appropriate representatives of the denomination to serve in specialized ministries. Both employers and professional certifying bodies look to religious endorsing bodies for this endorsement because:

- It attests to one's suitability for ministry in a particular setting;
- It gains the denomination's support for one's ministry beyond church walls;
- It provides an assurance the clergyperson is in good standing and appointable by the bishop; and
- It renders an affirmation the clergyperson will accommodate the religious rights of all persons within the institution or organization's scope of care.

If an individual moves from one setting to another, that person's endorsement will be reviewed and, if granted, will be issued for the new setting. From application to endorsement, the process normally takes two to four months.

Ecclesiastical approval is provided for certain civilian/volunteer settings (e.g., Civil Air Patrol, fire, police, crisis responder chaplaincies, etc.), organizational certifications and for seminary students who are seeking enrollment in the military chaplain candidate program. An ecclesiastical approval is not the same as an endorsement.

Requirements for Ecclesiastical Endorsement

People seeking ecclesiastical endorsement to a specific setting must meet the following criteria:
- Be a deacon, elder, provisional member, or associate member of an annual conference.
- Graduate from an accredited college and seminary.
- Complete additional requirements as specified by the setting.

Requirements for Ecclesiastical Approval

Local pastors who desire to serve in a ministry in a specialized setting may apply to the United Methodist Endorsing Agency for ecclesiastical approval status.

The Endorsement Process

- Contact the United Methodist Endorsing Agency (UMEA) via mail, phone, or e-mail to receive an application (www.gbhem. org/chaplains).
- Applicants are responsible for providing materials requested on the application form to UMEA.
- Provide names and addresses of two personal references and your district superintendent.
- Provide a life sketch and statement of ministry.
- Complete the interview process.

The Interview

- A central interviewing committee is made up of endorsed chaplains. Whenever possible, at least one member of the committee will represent the setting for which you seek endorsement.
- The purpose of this interview is to understand your perception of Christian faith as it relates to the setting in which you desire to minister.
- One member of the committee will serve as presenter for you and will be especially familiar with your materials in detail. You will be notified of the recommendation at the time of your interview.
- Following the interview, the committee will make a recommendation to the endorsing committee.
- The endorsing committee has the authority to grant or deny ecclesiastical endorsement. It is composed of members elected to the General Board of Higher Education and Ministry Board of Directors. The committee meets three times a year and has responsibility for policy and process regarding endorsement. Endorsement is valid only while you are under appointment to the setting for which endorsement was granted.

Change of Endorsed Settings

Contact UMEA if you change settings since a new endorsement may be required. Endorsement for chaplaincy does not guarantee employment or appointment. Employers establish criteria that the church does not influence. For example, maximum age limits for initial entry, physical fitness, and security clearances are three requirements that are set by the military departments. The Federal Bureau of Prisons has similar requirements. Other endorsements often require experience in the specialized setting and documentation as to effectiveness in that ministry. Others may require membership and certification in a pastoral care organization.

Endorsement for Deacons

There are four components of service as a chaplain: appointment, endorsement, certification, and employment. A deacon may be appointed to serve as a chaplain if the request for appointment is

Military chaplains go to all corners of the world to deliver rites and sacraments such as baptism to all who are in need and would otherwise be far from a local church.

approved by the bishop; if endorsement is granted; if the deacon is working toward certification; and, if an employer is willing to hire.

It is critical to understand that deacons have no sacramental authority unless granted by their bishop, and therefore, may not be eligible for all settings requiring endorsement. Deacons are eligible for endorsement to non-military settings and must meet the same requirements as elders: provisional or full conference membership, training, experience, and certification as appropriate. Endorsement to military settings is limited to elders due to the requirement for sacramental authority in those settings.

Civilian Chaplaincy

Standards for endorsement include relationship with and/or certification by the appropriate national professional pastoral care organization.

Those recognized include:

- American Association for Marriage and Family Therapy (AAMFT), www.aamft.org

- American Association on Intellectual and Developmental Disabilities (AAIDD), www.aaidd.org
- American Association of Pastoral Counselors (AAPC), www.aapc.org
- American Correctional Chaplains Association (ACCA), www.correctionalchaplains.org
- Association for Clinical Pastoral Education (ACPE), www.acpe.edu
- Association of Professional Chaplains (APC), www.professionalchaplains.org
- College of Pastoral Supervision and Psychotherapy (CPSP), www.cpsp.org
- Federation of Fire Chaplains (FFC), www.firechaplains.org
- International Coach Federation, www.coachfederation.org
- International Conference of Police Chaplains (ICPC), www.icpc4cops.org

Tammi Mott, a United Methodist from Unadilla, N.Y., helps to rebuild a home in the West Bank town of Anata.

- National Institute of Business & Industrial Chaplaincy (NIBIC), www.nibic.com
- National Association of Veterans Affairs Chaplains (NAVAC), www.navac.net
- Contact information is also available at the UMEA Web site: www.gbhem.org/chaplains or by calling 615-340-7411, or email: umea@gbhem.org.

In situations not covered by recognized certifying agencies, GBHEM will set minimum standards which may include specialized training for the type of ministry for which endorsement is sought and may include at least one year of supervised clinical training or comparable professional experience.

Civilian Endorsement Settings
- Children's Home
- Clinical Pastoral Education
- General Hospital
- Hospice
- Life Coach
- Marriage and Family Therapy
- Mental Health
- Pastoral Counseling
- Police
- Prison/Corrections
- Retirement Community
- Substance Abuse
- Veterans Affairs
- Workplace

Military Chaplaincy
Army: Active, Reserve, National Guard
Navy: Active, Reserve
Air Force: Active, Reserve, Air National Guard
Basic requirements for initial appointment to active duty or reserve:
- Be a citizen of the United States.
- Be physically qualified for general service based on an examination by the military.

- Meet current requirements determined by the military.

Applicants are responsible for contacting the military branch for which they are seeking endorsement. For military branch contact information, contact the United Methodist Endorsing Agency, www.gbhem.org/chaplains.

Steps Into Certification in Areas of Specialized Ministry

Certification in Christian education, youth ministry, music ministry, evangelism, camp and retreat ministry, older adult ministry, and spiritual formation by The United Methodist Church resulted from a desire of people in these fields to serve the church with excellence. It is available to qualifying lay people, deacons, elders, local pastors and diaconal ministers.

Certification is the church's recognition that an individual has met the required standards for academic training, experience, and continuing study necessary to achieve and maintain professional excellence in areas of specialized ministry.

The church's need for individuals who can serve to the best of their ability makes certification by The United Methodist Church increasingly important. For a current list of areas available for certification, visit www.gbhem.org/certification.

Graduate Certification

Certification is available to those who have completed a graduate degree in an area of specialization that includes approved core courses and to those who have an undergraduate degree and complete the core graduate courses for their specialized area. In both cases the courses must be taken at an institution approved by the General Board of Higher Education and Ministry.

Detailed steps for Certification in Areas of Specialized Ministry are posted at www.gbhem.org/certifcation.

Steps include:

- Make interest known to the certification registrar of the annual conference Board of Ordained Ministry.
- Enroll with GBHEM and the annual conference in the certification for specialized ministry process.

- Meet personal and church requirements as listed on the application form.
- Complete academic requirements including certification courses required for the specialized ministry area. Financial assistance is available for completion of certification courses.
- Complete two years of experience in the specialized ministry area.
- Apply for certification through www.gbhem.org/certification.
- Submit requested reference letters and complete background check and psychological assessment.
- Interview with the Board of Ordained Ministry to determine qualification for specialized ministry certification.

Undergraduate Certification

Certification is available to graduates from an undergraduate institution with a major in a specialized ministry area when the institution's program has been approved by the General Board of Higher Education and Ministry. For a list of these institutions, see the GBHEM website at www.gbhem.org/certification. After graduation these people must serve two years in their specialized ministry area before applying for certification.

Paraprofessional Certification

Paraprofessional certification is available to those working in areas of specialized ministry through programs approved by the General Board of Higher Education and Ministry. These programs are available through some jurisdictions, annual conferences, colleges, and seminaries. Paraprofessional certification does not have academic credit and is designed for people who are at least 35 years old and who have not had the opportunity to complete an undergraduate degree, and are seeking training in a specialized ministry.

To apply for Undergraduate or Paraprofessional Certification, meet the required steps as outlined above and detailed at www.gbhem.org/certification.

Chapter Four
Guidelines for Using the Text

As a deacon, elder, local pastor, chaplain, campus minister, or other United Methodist clergy, one of the most significant and satisfying tasks you have is to help identify, advise, and assist those called to servant leadership in our denomination. For many, this responsibility is not so much a task as it is the joy and satisfaction of relating to people and their deepest level of need at the time of a major vocational decision.

You can assist people exploring vocational options in many ways.

- Direct them to read this text, a vocational guide for service opportunities in The United Methodist Church.
- Meet with them and use *The Christian as Minister* as the basis of a series of conversations on the meaning of Christian vocation.
- Help them see beyond the seemingly impersonal, formal requirements for ministry in The United Methodist Church to the intention of the church to find the most effective people for its leadership.
- Help inquiring people examine a variety of leadership possibilities, receive feedback on their leadership potential, and test their leadership skills.
- Share insights about their family and background that will be

helpful to the individuals or to the committees that may consider them for ministerial service.

- Connect them with events in your annual conference, such as an Orientation to Ministry or a retreat that focuses on calling in order to provide more opportunities for discernment.

If you know of serious factors that may mean the individual should not be encouraged further in the exploration of a particular form of ministry, it is important that you discuss these with the individual. Regardless of the outcome of the inquiry, your concern is equally for the inquirer and the future leadership needs of the church.

Using The Christian as Minister as a Guide with Others

The Christian as Minister was written to assist you in helping others discern their vocational calling. The following suggestions may be helpful:

- Read through *The Christian as Minister* and participate in any training offered through the district Committee or conference Board of Ordained Ministry.
- As you become familiar with the contents, you will see various ways it can be used in the interpretation of God's call to ministry. You may also discover new information about the options for ministerial service, their standards and requirements.
- Order a supply of *The Christian as Minister* for your study, church library, office, or workplace.
- Use sections of *The Christian as Minister* with your Staff/Pastor-Parish Relations Committee, confirmation class, or any other group that wishes to study the meaning of Christian vocation.
- Give a copy to those you believe are considering a church related occupation and follow-up with regarding questions they may have about discerning their call.
- Visit www.explorecalling.org to learn more about identifying spiritual gifts.

- Help the committee to gain insight into a theology of ministry.
- Review the committee's responsibility for interviewing and recommending candidates for ordained and licensed ministry to the charge conference.
- Clarify the steps a candidate must take in order to enter ordained or licensed ministry.
- Discuss the resources the church can provide to assist a person who wishes to enter a church related occupation.
- Identify other resources available through the district, conference, or general agencies of the church that can assist as well.

Offer to counsel with those inquiring into church related occupations

- Explore the meaning of God's mission, Christ's call to servant leadership, an understanding of vocation, and the options for ministry in The United Methodist Church.
- Help the inquirers to see themselves as others see them and to appreciate the gifts and grace they bring to various vocational choices.
- Give them exposure to a variety of forms of ministry through research, observations, and interviewing.
- Help them to view a variety of options before making any commitments to further exploration.
- Once a tentative decision is made, clarify the steps to be taken in order to make that vocational choice a reality.

Maintain confidentiality

- Those inquiring into church-related occupations need the freedom to explore their vocational options without a premature disclosure of their intentions.
- Confidentiality is needed to prevent a premature commitment of a congregation to a candidate. When this occurs, there is

always the danger that an inquirer may respond by making a commitment to the wrong vocational choice, or perhaps the right choice for the wrong reasons.

- Confidentiality at the inquiring stage is also essential for those contemplating a career change. Unnecessary pressure is often brought to bear on an employee when it is discovered that she/ he is even thinking about changing careers.

Chapter Five
Guidelines for the Staff/Pastor-Parish Relations Committee

The enlistment, guidance, and support of candidates for ordained and licensed ministry in The United Methodist Church is not solely the responsibility of the clergy. It is shared with all laity as well with certain responsibilities assigned to the Staff/Pastor-Parish relations committee (S/P-PRC).

The responsibilities of the committee include enlisting, interviewing, evaluating, reviewing, and recommending candidates for licensed or ordained ministry or those applying for missionary service. The committee shares candidates' names with the charge conference and monitors progress on all those enrolled in the candidacy and ordination process.

For the sake of the candidates and the enhancement of ministry in The United Methodist Church, this responsibility of the S/P-PRC must not be taken lightly. Candidates need the affirmation and support of the committee in order to enter candidacy for ordained or licensed ministry. They need the resources an S/P-PRC can coordinate in the local church for those it recommends. Candidates will also benefit from regular contact with the committee as they prepare to meet the educational and other requirements of their vocational choice.

No one knows candidates better than the local church members. The S/P-PRC recommendation to the charge conference and, in turn, the charge conference's recommendation to the district Committee on Ordained Ministry is a critical step for all candidates to complete in order to enter ordained or licensed ministry. It is the one place where the *Discipline* requires the approval of the church's lay leadership in the candidacy selection process. It is the one opportunity the local church has to be sure that ministry candidates meet the criteria and expectations of the local church. If you are concerned about the quality of ministerial leadership in our denomination today, here is one place to address that need.

Finally, although the *Discipline* requires that only candidates for ordained or licensed ministry be enlisted, guided, and supported through the S/P-PRC, there is no reason why this committee cannot involve itself in the enlistment of persons for all forms of Christian service. If the committee, the pastor, and the administrative board/council so determine, the committee can have a significant impact on the way the local church looks at the matter of Christian vocation and the quality of people enlisted for all forms of church related service. Such a task that is done well not only affirms those identified as potential servant leaders, but broadens the vision of the congregation in terms of the nature of Christian vocation. It also awakens the church to the potential that exists for addressing the ministerial needs of the church and gives the local church the satisfaction of knowing that it is playing a significant role in the shaping of ministry for the future.

Guidelines for S/P-PRC Members

- Review *The Christian as Minister* with your pastor and other clergy staff, and, if necessary, clarify the role of the committee in the enlistment of candidates for ministry.
- Have the S/P-PRC chairperson meet with a candidate prior to the meeting where she/he will be interviewed in order to clarify the purpose of the meeting and the committee's expectations.

- If a written statement is to be prepared, communicate the format and the information that will be requested to the candidate.
- The meeting with the candidate may be informal and spontaneous. If the candidate is invited to make a brief oral statement of his/her current decision and interests, the committee members and the candidate may then be free to discuss any issues that seem important.
- While conducting an interview, the committee may wish to keep in mind the historic questions first asked by John Wesley in 1746. These questions apply to anyone seeking to enter candidacy for licensed or ordained ministry.

Candidates are interviewed in light of Wesley's Historic Questions as the S/P-PRC discerns the next steps in someone responding to a call to licensed or ordained ministry.

1) Do they know God as pardoning God? Have they the love of God abiding in them? Do they desire nothing but God? Are they holy in all manner of conversation?
2) Have they gifts, as well as evidence of God's grace, for the work? Have they a clear, sound understanding; a right judgment in the things of God; a just conception of salvation by faith? Do they speak justly, readily, clearly?
3) Have they fruit? Have any been truly convinced of sin and converted to God, and are believers edified by their service?

The decision of the S/P-PRC should be based on more than just the individual's appearance and presentation to the committee. It should also consider how well this person has done in the life of the local church over an extended period of time. This is the reason for the requirement of the candidate having been a member in good standing or a baptized and active participant of a local church or other United Methodist ministry setting for at least one year.

As the committee interviews a candidate for ministry, the following questions may be helpful:

- In what ways has this person actually experienced God's forgiveness and grace? Does this show in the way she/he lives? How?
- Does this person have personal habits that enhance his/her witness as a Christian? Which personal habits diminish or negate that witness?

- What gifts, skills, and abilities does this person have? Can she/he speak clearly and comfortably before a large group and in a small discussion group? What impression or feeling do you get from being with this person? Does this person seem positive, confident, poised, relaxed, open, and friendly?
- How does this person relate to his/her family? Are relatives (parents, siblings, spouse) supportive of the person's candidacy for ministry? Is this person being discouraged by some family members? Why? Do some family members seem to be pushing this person into some form of ministry as a career? In what ways?
- Does this person seem to have the intellectual ability (appropriate to his/her age) to study effectively and work with the Bible, theological issues, and the subject matter of the intended career? Has this person had relatively good grades in high school and college?
- How does this person relate to those in authority, such as church leaders, pastors, managers, teachers, employers, and others who supervise his/her work in some way? Is this person independent, assertive, yet cooperative and pleasant?
- What evidence of effectiveness in church-related leadership has this person already shown? Describe these. To what extent were these areas of effectiveness the result of this person's initiative and abilities, as compared to being someone else's work that this person merely followed or used?
- What other evidence of future potential has this person shown?
- How committed does this person seem to be to the gospel of Christ and servant ministry in The United Methodist Church? To what extent may salary, prestige, and other rewards be important to this person? How does she/he respond to discouragement, failure, disagreements, and other adverse conditions that are often part of ministry? Will this person be comfortable with the possible restrictions that ministry in the connectional structure of United Methodism may impose in some situations?
- What other evidence do you have that the person will enhance and improve the quality of ministry in The United Methodist Church?

Before a candidate is recommended to the charge conference, committee members, if they have not already done so, may invite informal, confidential comments from church members and others who know the applicant. If concerns are expressed about the applicant's fitness for ordained or licensed ministry, the S/P-PRC may want to delay making a recommendation to the charge conference until it has time to examine the comments and consult with the applicant about them.

When announcements are made that the charge conference will be voting on a recommendation of candidacy for ordained or licensed ministry, an open invitation should be given to any person who wishes to consult privately and confidentially with the pastor or S/P-PRC chairperson about the applicant. In this way it is more likely that varied points of view will be heard and any negative comments will be dealt with in a constructive way.

If potential problem areas do appear from any of these sources, the pastor and the S/P-PRC can decide how to use them in the most constructive manner with the applicant. It may be appropriate to consult with the person offering negative information, delay making a recommendation to the charge conference, or take other action prior to the conference if it is likely that the conference may not be able to handle the issues in a public meeting.

If the announcements of the meeting are made properly and if no serious issues become known that should be handled privately with the applicant, the charge conference meeting provides the public occasion when the church gives its formal endorsement of the applicant.

Charge Conference Recommendation

- The chairperson of the S/P-PRC will want to review and emphasize the importance of the decision facing the charge conference. Quoting from some of the *Disciplinary* statements or from the questions suggested for the S/P-PRC may reinforce the importance and the challenge of ordained or licensed ministry and charge conference's role.

- The chairperson may offer the candidate the opportunity to make a brief presentation to the conference as a way of introducing or renewing acquaintance with all those present.
- The chairperson of the S/P-PRC should then report on the committee's recommendation to the charge conference. The reasons for that recommendation should be spelled out in some detail.
- Time may be allowed for others to comment and present evidence that would support or deny the recommendation.
- The general tone and atmosphere of the conference meeting should be warm, relaxed, and flexible to allow for serious consideration of the decision.
- The charge conference, like the S/P-PRC must keep in mind these two objectives in its decision:
  1) To do what is in the best interest of The United Methodist Church and the enhancement of its ministry.
  2) To exhibit a pastoral concern for the individual, regardless of the outcome of the decision.

The S/P-PRC must consider ways to maintain its relationship with the candidates it affirms. Candidates for licensed or ordained ministry require an annual recommendation from the committee and the charge conference until they become local pastors or provisional members of the annual conference.

For further guidance in the work of the S/P-PRC with candidates for ministry, consult the *Guidelines for Leading Your Congregation: Pastor/Staff Parish Relations*, available from Cokesbury.

Appendix

United Methodist Schools of Theology

Boston University School of Theology
www.bu.edu/sth

Candler School of Theology, Emory University
www.candler.emory.edu

Claremont School of Theology
www.cst.edu

Drew Theological School
www.drew.edu/theo

The Divinity School, Duke University
www.divinity.duke.edu

Gammon Theological Seminary

www.gammonseminary.org

Garrett-Evangelical Theological Seminary

www.garrett.edu

Iliff School of Theology

www.iliff.edu

Methodist Theological School in Ohio

www.mtso.edu

Perkins School of Theology

www.smu.edu/perkins

Saint Paul School of Theology

www.spst.edu

United Theological Seminary

www.united.edu

Wesley Theological Seminary

www.wesleyseminary.edu

CPSIA information can be obtained
at www.ICGtesting.com
Printed in the USA
LVHW072125250119
605364LV00037B/407/P